MW00928944

I want to thank the editing and proofreading team: Donita Johnson, DMin, Pat Mora, and Kathy A. Kendrick

Ancient Prophecies from the Dead Sea Scrolls
by Ken Johnson, ThD

Printed in the United States of America

ISBN 9798321014738

Unless otherwise indicated, Bible quotations are taken from the Dead Sea Scrolls themselves.

The Essene Community

The Scrolls' Discovery Predicted

Church history records several factions of Jews in the first century. Among these were the Scribes, Pharisees, Sadducees, and Essenes. We didn't know much about the Essenes until the discovery of the Dead Sea Scrolls.

It is interesting that the discovery of the Dead Sea Scrolls seems to have been prophesied by Isaiah the prophet, and the very first Dead Sea Scroll to come into Israeli hands was the Great Isaiah Scroll (1QIsa). A professor purchased that first scroll on the very day that Israel became a state in AD 1948. Also amazing is that the Temple Scroll and the Damascus Document came into Israeli hands during the Six Day War (AD 1967)—the war which resulted in Israel taking control of the Temple Mount! These facts cannot be a coincidence. Notice how the prophet Isaiah describes this:

> Woe to Ariel, to Ariel, the city where David dwelt! Add ye year to year; let them kill sacrifices. Yet I will distress Ariel, and there shall be heaviness and sorrow: and it shall be unto Me as Ariel. And I will camp against thee round about, and will lay siege against thee with a mount, and I will raise forts against thee. And thou shalt be brought down … (Isaiah 29:1–4a KJV)

In this first part, God is angry with Israel. He sides with the invaders to cause the nation of Israel to be "brought down" or scattered. This started in AD 70 with the destruction of the Jerusalem Temple. It ended with the destruction of the Bar Kokhba rebellion in AD 135. During this time, the Essenes hid the Dead Sea Scrolls in caves around the Qumran area. After this, in AD 135, the next part of Isaiah 29:4 would occur.

> ... and shalt speak out of the ground, and thy speech shall be low out of the dust; and thy voice shall be, as of one that hath a familiar spirit, out of the ground, and thy speech shall whisper out of the dust.
> (Isaiah 29:4b KJV)

There is only one way the ancients, who are dead (ghosts), could speak to us today. That is by finding their records in the dust of the ground where they buried them. So, when were their records discovered? In the war described by the very next verses of Isaiah:

> Moreover, the multitude of thy strangers shall be like small dust, and the multitude of the terrible ones shall be as chaff that passeth away: yea, it shall be at an instant suddenly. Thou shalt be visited of the Lord of Hosts with thunder, and with earthquake, and great noise, with storm and tempest, and the flame of devouring fire. And the multitude of all the nations that fight against Ariel, even all that fight against her and her munition, and that distress her, shall be as a dream of a night vision. (Isaiah 29:5–7 KJV)

Notice that in this war, God is fighting *for* Israel and *against* a coalition of nations, which He destroys. This is a different war than the one in AD 70–135 in which God fought *against* Israel and allowed Rome to destroy them. This Isaiah 29 war starts because the Jews return to form the modern nation of Israel. So, AD 1948 started a period when Israel began to find scrolls from their ancient forefathers and regain much of the knowledge that had been lost to them.

The prophet Daniel also predicted that, toward the End Times, many people would be running "to and fro." They would be seeking something that increases knowledge.

> And they that be wise shall shine as the brightness of the firmament; and they that turn many to righteousness as the stars for ever and ever. But thou, O Daniel, shut up the words, and seal the book, even to the time of the end: many shall run to and fro, and knowledge shall be increased. (Daniel 12:3–4)

Church father Irenaeus said this prophecy from Daniel would be fulfilled when the Jews returned to restore the State of Israel.

> Daniel the prophet says, "Shut up the words and seal the book even to the time of consummation, until many learn, and knowledge be completed. For at that time, when the dispersion shall be accomplished, they shall know all these things."
> (Irenaeus, *Against Heresies* 4.26, AD 170)

Combining history with Daniel, Isaiah, and Irenaeus, we see that the Essene teachings were to be hidden until the nation of Israel returned. After AD 1948, knowledge would increase when people would run "to and fro" in archaeological digs, discovering ancient scrolls and reading what the ancients taught.

The Essene Calendar: 4Q252–254

While not prophetic, the Essene calendar solves many problems dealing with chronology. The Essenes taught that the day of the creation of the sun, moon, and stars began the calendar year. That was day four of Creation Week. Adam was created on day six. The Essenes believed the weekly cycle was unbroken up to their time. Thus, God created Adam on day six, the first Friday afternoon. After 130 years had passed since the creation of Adam (with no gaps in time), Seth was born, and so on. The Essene calendar has periods of time called "Ages," which are each 2,000 years. The Age of Creation was from Creation (ca 3925 BC on our calendar) to the Call of Abraham, when he was 52, in 1926 BC. The Age of Torah was from Abraham to AD 75. The Age of Grace began in AD 76 and will end at the beginning of the Kingdom Age in AD 2075. Then the Kingdom Age will last only 1,000 years. The Essenes numbered the years in sets of Jubilees, or 50-year periods. Ten Jubilees equaled one *Onah*, or one 500-year period. There would be 14 Onahs (140 Jubilees) between the creation of Earth and the creation of a new heavens and a new Earth, comprising their 7,000-year prophetic timeline.

Dead Sea Scroll 11Q13 says the Messiah's death would occur toward the end of Onah 8, one *Shemittah* (seven-year period) after the end of the ninth Jubilee. That is AD 32 on our calendar, placing the last Jubilee of the Age of Grace at AD 2026–2075. The last Jubilee of an age is sometimes

9

called the *last generation* in the scrolls. Many ancients and church fathers thought the year 6000 AM (*anno mundi*; i.e., year since the creation of the world) would be the start of the "Kingdom Age," which we call the Millennium. There are reasons why we can use this logic to see the *season* of His return but not identify any *specific dates* for it.

The Essenes taught that we should be aware of the correct calendar and the appointed times of the festivals, e.g., Passover and Pentecost. The symbols embedded in the rituals performed on these festivals teach prophecy. For example, we know that the Passover Seder shows the death, burial, and resurrection of the Messiah. We know the Gospels state that Jesus died on Passover and that the church was born on Pentecost. Many believe His Second Coming is seen in the fall festivals. See my book, *Ancient Messianic Festivals*, for a detailed study on these.

Regarding the appointed times, the scrolls state,

> Add knowledge of the *appointed times*, the meanings of which I will explain, so that you will be ready for the *End of the Ages*, and study the former things [written Testaments] so that you will know when that Day dawns.[1] (4Q298, Fragments 3 and 4)

The scrolls also indicate that most prophecies are fulfilled during the turn of the Ages:

> Always at the genesis of every *Onah*, at the beginning of every Age, and at the end of every

---

[1] Compare this to 2 Peter 1:19, the rising of the Day Star in our hearts.

season, according to the statute, signs are appointed to every dominion.[2] (Hymn 23)

The holy weeks [*Shemittahs*], appointed times, heads of the months [*Tekufahs*], head of the years, the glorious festival seasons, all in their fixed times, teach the Sabbatical years of the land and the divisions of the appointed times for liberty and bondage, for light and darkness... (4Q286)

In the last Jubilee of the Age of Creation, Nimrod's tower fell. This began the destruction of Nimrod's antichrist system and religion. In the last Jubilee of the Age of Torah, the Messiah brought the gift of salvation, and the Church was born. If this pattern continues, sometime in the last Jubilee of the Age of Grace, we should see the destruction of the Antichrist, the crushing of Belial (Satan), and the institution of the Kingdom Age.

At the end of that Jubilee ... He will rebuke Belial ... in these days her enemies will ... (4Q462)

At the completion of that Jubilee, He will rebuke Belial ... (4Q463)

Our book, *Ancient Book of Jubilees*, has an entire chapter on how the Jews forsook their God-given calendar for a corrupted one. They started performing festivals and sacrifices on the wrong days. The Dead Sea Scroll 4Q306,

---

[2] This seems to indicate there are more movements of God, miracles, and prophecies fulfilled around the changes of the *Onahs* and Ages than at other times. The use of the word "dominion" seems to indicate this rather than saying the Essenes marked the beginning and end of the times.

called "Men of Error," prophesied that the sons of Levi would corrupt the calendar:

> Their descendants who will stray and not observe the commandments will transgress day to day and month to month. (4Q306, Fragment 1)

We produced the book, *The Ancient Dead Sea Scroll Calendar*, which gives a more complete picture of the 364-day calendar and its leap-week system.

To show how accurate the Essene calendar is, let's look at the "Genesis Commentary," 4Q252–254. This covers Genesis chapters 6–8. Square brackets denote my comments.

> Their end began in the 480th year of Noah's life when God said, "My spirit will not always strive with man forever." They had 120 years until the time of the waters of the Flood [to repent]. And the waters of the Flood came upon the earth in the 600th year of Noah's life, on the seventeenth day of the second month, the first day of the week [Sunday, Iyar 17, 1656 AM], and there was rain upon the earth for forty days and forty nights, until the twenty-sixth day of the third month, the fifth day of the week [Thursday, Sivan 26]. The waters swelled upon the earth for 150 days, until the fourteenth day of the seventh month, which was the third day of the week [Tuesday, Tishrei 14].
> (4Q252, Column 1, Fragments 1 and 2)

This first fragment shows that the 120-year period was not a prophecy about a decrease in lifespan. It was a prophecy about the coming judgment if people did not repent. This means that the people of the time knew the exact day (or at least year) of the judgment and still ignored the warning.

If we count the years in the genealogy from Genesis 5, we can calculate the year of the Flood as being 1,656 years from Creation, or the year 1656 AM. (Again, AM is the abbreviation for *anno mundi*, meaning the year since the creation of the world. AD is an abbreviation for *anno domini*, meaning the year of our Lord. AM dates start at Creation, and AD dates start at the birth of Christ.)

Now, look at this verse about the days of the year:

> In the six hundredth year of Noah's life, in the second month, the seventeenth day of the month, the same day were all the fountains of the great deep broken up, and the windows of heaven were opened. (Genesis 7:11 KJV)

That is pretty specific. Creation was in the spring, as the Essenes teach. The first month was Nisan, and the second month was Iyar. That gives us a date of Iyar 17 for the Flood. But if their seven-day-week cycle is truly unbroken, the date of the Flood would be Sunday, Iyar 17, 1656 AM. I had always wondered why specific dates like that were not recorded. Now, we know that they were. But the Pharisees realized that this made it just too easy to pinpoint when the Messiah came. This text goes on:

> At the end of the 150 days, the waters decreased for two days, the fourth and fifth days. And on the sixth

day, the Ark came to rest on the mountains of Ararat; it was the seventeenth day of the seventh month [Friday, Tishrei 17]. The water continued to decrease until the tops of the mountains became visible on the first day of the tenth month, the fourth day of the week [Wednesday, Tevet 1; the winter Day of Remembrance]. Then Noah opened the window of the Ark, on the tenth day of the eleventh month, the first day of the week [Sunday, Shevat 10]. And he sent the dove to see if the waters had abated, but it did not find a resting place and came back to him and the ark. He waited another seven days, and he sent it out again, and it came back to him with newly plucked leaves of an olive tree in its beak. This was the twenty-fourth day of the eleventh month, on the first day of the week [Sunday, Shevat 24]. Then Noah knew that the waters had abated from the earth. Another seven days later, he sent forth the dove, and it did not return. This was the first day of the twelfth month, on the first day of the week [Sunday, Adar 1]. Thirty-one days after the dove was sent and did not return, the waters were dried up from upon the earth. Noah removed the covering of the ark to look, and he saw the surface of the ground had dried up. This was the first day of the first month, which was on the fourth day of the week [Wednesday, Nisan 1, 1657 AM]. (4Q252, Column 1, Fragments 1 and 2)

We should compare the dates for these events to festivals, because they may have a prophetic meaning.

The scrolls go on to explain,

> On the seventeenth day of the second month, in the
> six hundred and first year of Noah's life, the earth
> was dried up. This was the first day of the week
> [Sunday, Iyar 17, 1657 AM]. On this day, Noah went
> forth from the ark at the end of a complete year of
> 364 days. On the first day of the week [Sunday], in
> the seventh ... one and six ... Noah from the ark at
> the appointed time, a complete year ... And Noah
> awoke from his wine and knew what his youngest
> son had done to him. And he said, "cursed be
> Canaan! A slave of slaves will he be to his brothers."
> He did not curse Ham, but his son, because God
> blessed the sons of Noah ... and "in the tents of Shem
> may He dwell ..." A land He gave to Abram, His
> friend. Terah was 140 years old when he left Ur of
> the Chaldees and entered Haran. And Abram was 70
> years old. And for five years, Abram stayed in Haran.
> And after he left ... the land of Canaan, sixty ... the
> heifer, ram, and goat ... Abram for ... the fire when
> it passed ... at Abram's departure ... Canaan ...
> (4Q252, Column 2, Fragments 1 and 3)

> The dove ... and this is the computation of the
> making of the ark; three hundred cubits is the length
> of the ark, fifty cubits is its width, and thirty cubits
> ... and the measurement of the ark ... Noah went out
> from the ark at the appointed time, year by year ...
> the raven and it went out and returned to make known
> to later generations that ... before Him and because
> the raven had gone forth and had returned. (4Q254a)

The main reason for adding the "Genesis Commentary" here is to show the accuracy of the calendar. In the chapter on 11Q13, we will see that the Essenes taught that the Messiah would be God incarnate, would die for our sins, and would reconcile us to the Father in AD 32. You can't get more accurate than that!

Qumran Beliefs

We need to have a basic understanding of the Essenes' world view before we look at the newly discovered ancient prophecies in the Dead Sea Scrolls.

The Essenes believed in Genesis as literal history. They also believed the 10 pre-flood and 10 post-flood patriarchs were prophets. These prophets wrote what they called Testaments. These were a kind of last will and testament giving instructions to their children for generations to come. They contain very personal family stories, moral lessons, and prophecy. These Testaments were collected and made into a kind of pre-mosaic canon.

From Genesis 5, we have a list of the 10 pre-flood patriarchs:

Adam, Seth, Enos, Cainan, Mahalaleel, Jared, Enoch, Methuselah, Lamech, and Noah.

The post flood patriarchs, down to Abraham, are listed in Genesis 11:10–26:

Shem, Arpachshad, Salah, Eber, Peleg, Reu, Serug, Nahor, Terah, and Abram.

The lineage continues:

Isaac, Jacob (Israel), Levi, Kohath, Amram, and Aaron (Moses's brother).

The Essenes believed that each one of these patriarchs wrote a Testament. Each patriarch collected all the previous Testaments and passed them down to their children. The Levitical priests were to keep this written library of scrolls.

Josephus's *Antiquities* 1 records that Adam gave a prophecy about the destruction of the world by a flood of water and another prophecy about the destruction of the world by fire. In that same chapter, Josephus also records that Seth had written about the calendar. The *Ancient Book of Jasher*, chapter 2, records that Cainan correctly understood Adam's prophecy and added it to his collection of scrolls. We do not (yet) have any of these particular Testaments from the Dead Sea Scrolls, but we do have a fragment of the "Testament of Enos." So, putting all this together, we know that the Testaments of Adam, Seth, Enos, and Cainan (the first four) did, indeed, exist. I wrote *Ancient Testaments of the Patriarchs*, which is a collection of all the Testaments that I know of that still exist. Hopefully, we will find more soon.

The Essenes teach that Jacob broke up the Melchizedekian priesthood—which was prophet, priest, and king combined—into three separate offices. From then on, the kings of Israel would come only through the line of Judah, and the priesthood would only come from the line of Levi. Levi kept the records until the predicted apostasy entered the priesthood.

From the time of Moses, there also began a School of the Prophets. Church father Hippolytus recorded the lineage of prophets who ran the school. You can find his entire commentary in the *Ante-Nicene Fathers* published by Eerdmans Publishing. It is a ten-volume encyclopedia of writings from the ancient church, covering the period from the time of Christ through AD 325. Hippolytus's work is in volume 5. He introduced the list of prophets by saying:

> These following are the names of the teachers who handed down the Law in continuous succession after Moses the prophet, until the advent of Messiah: God delivered the most excellent Law into the hands of Moses the prophet, the son of Amram.
> (*Hippolytus's Fragments on the Pentateuch*)

Here is his list:

1. Moses
2. Joshua
3. Othniel
4. Jehud
5. Shamgar
6. Baruk
7. Gideon
8. Abimelech
9. Taleg
10. Babin
11. Jephthah
12. Ephran
13. Elul

14. Abdon
15. Samson
16. Elkanah (father of Samuel the prophet)
17. Eli the priest
18. Samuel the prophet
19. Nathan the prophet
20. Gad the prophet
21. Shemaiah the teacher
22. Iddo the teacher
23. Ahijah the Shilonite
24. Abihu
25. Elijah the prophet
26. Elisha the prophet
27. Micah the prophet
28. Abdiahu
29. Jehuda
30. Zacharias the teacher
31. Esaia the prophet (the son of Amos)
32. Jeremiah the prophet
33. Ezekiel
34. Hosea the prophet (the son of Bazi)
35. Joel the prophet
36. Amos the prophet
37. Obadiah
38. Jonah the prophet (son of Mathi, the son of Armelah, who was the brother of Elias the prophet)
39. Micah the Morasthite
40. Nahum the Alcusite
41. Habakkuk the prophet

42. Zephaniah the prophet
43. Haggai the prophet
44. Zechariah the prophet (the son of Bershia)
45. Malachi
46. Ezra the teacher
47. Shamai the chief priest
48. Jaduah
49. Samean
50. Antigonus
51. Joseph (son of Johezer) and Joseph (the son of Gjuchanan)
52. Jehosua (son of Barachia)
53. Nathan the Arbelite
54. Simeon (elder son of Shebach who was also the Simeon who held the Messiah in his arms)
55. Jehuda
56. Zechariah the priest (father of John the Baptist)
57. Joseph (a teacher of the tribe of Levi)
58. Annas and Caiaphas

Because Annas and Caiaphas later became apostates, Mosaic Law gives the office back to Joseph (number 57) or one of his sons; but he had already died childless. So, the office would then go back to Zechariah or one of his sons. Zechariah had already been put to death by the corrupt priesthood. The honor of being the forerunner of the Messiah then fell to Zechariah's one and only son, John the Baptist. Other writings of church history state that, from that time on, the spiritual gift of prophecy *only occurred among Christians.*

Considering all this information, we should not only look for any Testaments from the original patriarchs but also watch for any prophecy books from the leaders of the School of the Prophets. We do know the whereabouts of the writings of five of these leaders, numbers 19–23, from Hippolytus's list:

> Nathan the prophet, Gad the prophet, Shemaiah the teacher, Iddo the teacher, and Ahijah the Shilonite.

Compare this list of five leaders with the following Bible verses, and we will see they did, indeed, write books of prophecy.

> Now the acts of David the king, first and last, behold, they are written in the book of Samuel the seer, and in the book of Nathan the prophet, and in the book of Gad the seer. (1 Chronicles 29:29 KJV)

> Now the acts of Rehoboam, first and last, are they not written in the book of Shemaiah the prophet, and of Iddo the seer concerning genealogies? And there were wars between Rehoboam and Jeroboam continually. (2 Chronicles 12:15 KJV)

> Now the rest of the acts of Solomon, first and last, are they not written in the book of Nathan the prophet, and in the prophecy of Ahijah the Shilonite, and in the visions of Iddo the seer against Jeroboam the son of Nebat? (2 Chronicles 9:29 KJV)

James H. Charlesworth wrote *The Old Testament Pseudepigrapha*. In volume 1, in the section on the Syriac version of Daniel, he states that there were reports that copies of these lost five were found among the earlier discovered Dead Sea Scrolls. If this is true, those writings are in the hands of private collectors. But at least that means they exist, and we may read them one day.

Prophetic Commentaries

Genesis Commentary: 4Q252–4

4Q252, Column 5

The scepter shall not depart from the tribe of Judah
... (Genesis 49:10)

Interpretation: While Israel has self-rule, there will not be anyone cut off who sits on the throne of David, for "the staff" represents the covenant of kingship, and "the standards" are the thousands of Israel, until the Messiah of Righteousness comes, the Branch of David [Isa. 11:1–2; Zech. 3:8], for to David and his sons have been given the covenant of the kingship of His people for everlasting generations, which he kept ... the Law with the men of the community, for ... it is the Congregation of the men of ... Nathan.

4Q254, Fragments 5–6: Antichrist Text... the two sons of oil who ... keepers of God's commandments ... for the men of the community ...

...and bowed his shoulder to bear and became a servant unto tribute. (Genesis 49:15)

Which ... the great ... a slave ...

Dan shall judge his people, as one of the tribes of Israel. Dan shall be a serpent by the way, an adder in the path, that biteth the horse heels, so that his rider shall fall backward. (Genesis 49:16–17)

Israel ...

Ken's Commentary

This text above, from 4Q252, shows a quote of Scripture and then the Essene commentary. What I find fascinating is that they taught that when the self-rule of Israel ceased, the Messiah would come. Even under control by a foreign power, Israel still had kings until Rome replaced the Jewish kings with King Herod. In Herod's days, the Messiah was born. In the future, the government will be turned over to the Messiah and His sons. The "sons" of Christ are "men of the Community," the Christians who will rule and reign with Him in the Kingdom.

The text of 4Q252 also hints at a prophecy from the "Testament of Nathan" (see 2 Chronicles 9:29). One of the fragments we have from Nathan's Testament predicts the Messiah's virgin birth.

> I saw one, a maiden and without touch of man, and a man-child in her arms, and that was the Lord of the earth unto the ends of the earth.
> (Fragment of *The Book of Nathan the Prophet*)

The second text, 4Q254, mentions the two "Sons of Oil." Zechariah refers to the two witnesses as Sons of Oil, or anointed ones.

> These are the two sons of fresh oil who stand by the Lord of the whole earth. (Zechariah 4:14 LITV)

I hope that we will find the ritual for the Festival of New Oil. Like the Passover Seder, it would explain a lot of prophecy to us. New Oil is most likely a reference to prophets or fulfilled prophecy. Scroll 4Q254 is called the

"Antichrist Text" because of the last section. There has never been a person from the tribe of Dan ruling Israel since Samson. It looks like 4Q254 teaches that, during the time of the two "Sons of New Oil," there will be an Antichrist that is somehow connected with the tribe of Dan. Several early church fathers teach that the Antichrist will either be born a Danite or born in the area that used to be occupied by the tribe of Dan. Today, that area is partly northern Israel and partly southern Syria.

Psalm 37 Commentary: 4Q171

He shall bring forth your righteousness as the light and your justice as the noonday. (Psalm 37:6)

Interpretation: … grace … boasting in the burning of … lovers of long locks, and seducers … wickedness by the hand of God.

Be silent before the Lord and long for Him, and be not upset against the successful, the man who achieves his plans. (Psalm 37:7a)

Interpretation: This concerns the Liar who led astray many with his lying words so that they seek smooth things instead of following the interpreter of knowledge … they shall perish by the sword, famine, and plague.

Relent from anger and abandon wrath. Do not be angry; it tends only to evil, for the wicked shall be cut off. (Psalm 37:8–9a)

Interpretation: This concerns all those who repent from their evil and return to the true Law. For all those who stubbornly refuse to repent from their iniquity shall be cut off.

But those who wait for the Lord shall possess the land. (Psalm 37:9b)

Interpretation: This is the congregation of His Elect who follow His will.

> A little while and the wicked shall be no more; I will look towards his place, but he shall be gone.
> (Psalm 37:10)

Interpretation: This concerns all the wicked. At the end of the <u>forty years,</u> they shall be blotted out, and the wicked shall no longer be found in the land of Israel.

> But the humble shall possess the land and delight in abundant peace. (Psalm 37:11)

Interpretation: This concerns the Congregation of the Humble who shall accept the season of repentance and shall be delivered from all the snares of Belial. Afterwards, all who inherit the earth shall delight and prosper in peace and prosperity.

> The wicked plots against the righteous and gnashes his teeth at him. The Lord laughs at him, for He sees that his day is coming. (Psalm 37:12–13)

Interpretation: This concerns the violent of the Covenant who are in the House of Judah/Jacob, who have plotted to destroy those who practice the true Law, who are in the Council of the Community. And God will not forsake them to their hands.

> The wicked draw the sword and bend their bow to bring down the poor and needy and to slay the upright of way. Their sword shall enter their own heart and their bows shall be broken.
> (Psalm 37:14–15)

Interpretation: This concerns the wicked of Ephraim and Manasseh, who shall seek to lay hands on the Priest and the men of His council at the Time of Trial which shall come upon them. But God will redeem them from out of their hand. And afterwards, they [the wicked] shall be delivered into the hand of the violent Gentiles [Rome] for judgement.

> Better is the little which the righteous has than the abundance of many wicked people. (Psalm 37:16)

Interpretation: This concerns those who practice the true Law, who refuse their evil.

> For the arms of the wicked shall be broken, but the Lord upholds the righteous. The Lord knows the days of the perfect, and their portion shall be forever. (Psalm 37:17–18)

Interpretation: This concerns the men of His grace …

> In evil times, they shall not be shamed. (Psalm 37:19a)

Interpretation: The repentant of the desert, who are saved, shall live for a thousand generations. All the glory of Adam shall belong to them and to their seed forever.

> And in the days of famine, they shall be satisfied, but the wicked shall perish. (Psalm 37:19b–20a)

Interpretation: God will keep them alive during the famine and the Time of Trouble. Many others shall perish from famine and plague, all those who have not departed from them to become part of the Congregation of His Elect.

> And those who love the Lord shall be like the pride of pastures. (Psalm 37:20b)

Interpretation: This concerns the Congregation of His Elect, who shall be leaders and princes of the flock among their herds.

> Like smoke they shall all of them vanish away. (Psalm 37:20c)

Interpretation: This concerns the princes of wickedness who have oppressed His holy people, and who shall perish like smoke blown away by the wind.

> The wicked borrow and do not repay, but the righteous are generous and give. Truly, those whom He blesses shall possess the land, but those whom He curses shall be cut off. (Psalm 37:21–22)

Interpretation: This concerns the Congregation of the Humble, who shall possess the whole earth as an inheritance. They shall possess the High Mountain of Israel forever and shall enjoy eternal delights in His Sanctuary. But the violent of the nations and the wicked of Israel shall be cut off and blotted out forever.

> The steps of the man are confirmed by the Lord and He delights in all his ways; though he stumbles, he shall not fall, for the Lord shall support his hand. (Psalm 37:23–24)

Interpretation: This concerns the Priest, the Teacher of Righteousness, whom God commanded to arise. He established Him to build for Himself the Congregation of the Humble, and His ways are true.

> I have been young and now am old, yet I have not seen the righteous forsaken, or his children begging

for bread. He is ever giving liberally and lending, and his children become a blessing. (Psalm 37:25–26)

Interpretation: This concerns the Teacher of Righteousness … Judgment.

The unjust shall be destroyed forever, and the children of the wicked shall be cut off. (Psalm 37:28)

Interpretation: These are the violent … the Law.

The righteous shall possess the land and dwell upon it forever. (Psalm 37:29)

Interpretation: This concerns … in a thousand generations.

The mouth of the righteous utters wisdom and his tongue speaks justice. The law of God is in his heart; his steps will not slip. (Psalm 37:30–31)

Interpretation: This concerns … of the truth which speaks … justice … to them.

The wicked watches out for the righteous and seeks to kill him. The Lord will not abandon him into his hand or let him be condemned when he is tried. (Psalm 37:32–33)

Interpretation: This concerns the Wicked Priest who watched the Teacher of Righteousness to kill Him because of the ordinance and the law which He sent to him. But God will not abandon Him nor condemn Him when He is tried. And [God] will pay him his reward by delivering him into the hand of the violent of the nations, that they may execute judgement upon him.

> Wait for the Lord and keep to His way, and He will exalt you to possess the land; you will look on the destruction of the wicked. (Psalm 37:34)

Interpretation: This concerns ... who will see the judgement of wickedness and with His Elect will rejoice in the heritage of truth.

> I have seen the wicked man overbearing like a cedar of Lebanon. He passed away and he was no more, though I looked for him, he could not be found. (Psalm 37:35–36)

Interpretation: This concerns the Liar who, against the Elect of God, sought to bring to an end ... behave with presumptuous arrogance.

> Mark the blameless man and the upright, for there is posterity for the man of peace. (Psalm 37:37)

Interpretation: This concerns ... peace.

> But the transgressors shall be altogether destroyed; the posterity of the wicked shall be cut off. (Psalm 37:38)

Interpretation: This concerns ... will perish and be cut off from the midst of the Congregation of the Community.

> But the salvation of the righteous is of the LORD: He is their strength in the Time of Trouble. He delivers them from the wicked and saves them because they take refuge in Him. (Psalm 37:39–40)

Interpretation: This concerns ... God will save them and deliver them from the wicked ones of ...

> To the chief musician: according to the lilies. For the
> sons of Korah. Maskil. A song of love (Psalm 45:1a)

Its interpretation is that they are the <u>seven divisions</u> of the
repentant of Israel ...

> My heart is stirred with a good word. I will speak of
> my work to the King. (Psalm 45:1b)

Interpretation: ... the Holy Spirit for ... books of ...

> And my tongue is the pen of a ready scribe.
> (Psalm 45:1)

Interpretation: This concerns the <u>Teacher of Righteousness</u>
... God with an answering tongue ...

Ken's Commentary

Psalm 37 verses 6–7 describe that the "Seekers of Smooth
Things," a term for the Sadducees, will corrupt everything
and cause destruction. They were, indeed, destroyed by
Titus's destruction of the Jerusalem Temple in AD 70.
Notice that there was one particular Sadducee leader
referred to as the Liar. This Liar refused to follow the
Messiah.

Verses 8–9 state all will be able to understand the true Way
of the Messiah and, when He comes, we must then turn
from our corrupt denominations (Pharisees, Sadducees,
etc.) and become followers of the Way (Christianity).
Those who love Messiah will follow His will.

Amazingly, verses 10–11 state that *40 years* after the
Messiah's death, the cultic Sadducees and Pharisees will

be destroyed. Jesus died in AD 32; and in AD 70, the temple was destroyed.

Verse 11 states that those who repent join the Congregation of the Poor (or humble). They must be careful during the 40-year season of repentance. This is the time allowed for the Sadducees and Pharisees to repent. Afterward will come the destruction of all who do not repent. After the 40-year period, Christians will not have to worry about being put into prison by Jewish leaders, for they will all be gone.

Verse 12–13 state that the violent (Sadducee-type leaders) will plot to destroy believers during the 40-year period, but God will protect them. At the end of that 40-year period, He will destroy the violent. The "Council of the Humble" are those who are non-violent and follow God's will, the true law, instead of their own desires.

Verses 14–17 state that the wicked plotted to kill the Messiah (the True Priest) and His followers. God protected His followers and used the Romans to destroy Israel. The "repentant of the desert" is a reference to the Essene Community who awaited the Messiah in the wilderness areas away from the corrupt leaders. Ephraim and Manasseh were tribes that separated from the nation as a whole. These became idioms, just like the "House of Separation." These terms refer to those who leave the true Way and join a cult, especially those who become violent.

Verses 18–20 state God protected those who believed and followed His instruction. Eusebius records that the prophets declared destruction was coming and that the Christians should leave Israel and travel to Pella. Believers did exactly that. Within days of their departure, Rome descended on Israel and slaughtered thousands of people. We must take prophecy literally and seriously!

Verses 23–24 teach that the Messiah, the Teacher of Righteousness, would die and rise again. He would then create His own congregation or Church.

Verses 25–31 don't have enough words to clearly understand the interpretation.

Verses 32–33 relate that the Liar, or Wicked Priest, watched for a time and way to kill the Messiah because of His teaching. The Messiah was condemned by the Liar and executed, but that judgment did not stand. The Messiah resurrected.

Verses 34–40 don't have enough words to clearly understand the interpretation.

Psalm 45, verses 1–2 have the maskil, or prophetic teaching, set to music. The melody is a tune called *To the Lilies*. The Hebrew word for lilies can also be translated "trumpets." Many have speculated that this might be a psalm about the time of the Rapture. The Essene commentary related this psalm to seven divisions of repentant people. This may be referring to the seven thousand years. The Targum of this psalm said that it's a prophecy about King Messiah.

Psalms 127, 129, and 118
Commentary: 4Q173

It is vain for you to rise early and lie down late. You shall eat the bread of toil; He shall feed those who love Him in their sleep. (Psalms 127:2)

Interpretation: They shall seek ... supplications from the Teacher of Righteousness ... priest at the end of the Age ...

Lo, sons are a heritage of the LORD. (Psalm 127:3)

Interpretation: Those who take possession of the inheritance ...

and the fruit of the womb is His reward.
(Psalm 127:3)

Interpretation: The "fruit" is the Teacher of Righteousness ...

Happy is the man that hath his quiver full of them: they shall not be ashamed, but they shall speak with the enemies in the gate. (Psalm 127:5)

Interpretation: They will be a congregation ... They will not be ashamed when they speak with enemies at the gate ...

The reaper does not fill his hand; nor he that binds sheaves his bosom. Neither do they which go by say, the blessing of the LORD be upon you: we bless you in the name of the LORD. (Psalm 129:7–8)

Interpretation: ...

> Blessed be he that comes in the name of the LORD:
> we have blessed you out of the house of the LORD.
> God is the LORD, who has showed us light: Bind the
> sacrifice with cords, even unto the horns of the altar.
> (Psalm 118:26–27)

Interpretation: ... pass over from the House of Stumbling
... unto the horns of the altar ... they will come ... this is
the gate of God which the righteous will enter though it ...
those who widen the waste places and desolate places ...

Ken's Commentary

My guess is that 4Q173 is saying the Messiah, Teacher of
Righteousness, is the true Priest at the end of the Age of
Torah. Psalm 127:5 is often thought of as a verse about
having biological children; but, as we see, the Essenes said
we should be focused on making many converts for Christ.

Psalm 129 seems to indicate that everyone should reject the
House of Stumbling, which is the Sadducee and Pharisee
cults who rejected the Messiah. Everyone should repent
and come back to the original teachings of Moses and
accept the Messiah.

The first-century Church constantly referred to the "door
of Jesus," meaning He is the only way of salvation. I
wonder if they took that phrase from this passage. Jesus is
the "door" or "gate" to enter salvation.

Isaiah Commentary: 4Q161–5, 4Q183

> I will remove its hedge that it may be burned; I will
> break down its wall that it may be trampled. I will lay
> it waste. It shall not be pruned or dug. There shall
> come up briers and thorns. (Isaiah 5:5–6)

Interpretation: He forsakes them. "There shall come up
briers and thorns" means the Way of Truth will be hidden
from their eyes.

> For the vineyard of the Lord of Hosts is the house of
> Israel, And the men of Judah are His pleasant plant.
> He looked for justice, but behold, oppression; For
> righteousness, but behold, a cry for help. (Isaiah 5:7)

Interpretation: The phrase "behold, a cry" concerns the End
of Days, at the doom of the earth *before* the sword and
famine; and it shall be in the time of the earth's visitation.

> Woe to those who rise early in the morning, that they
> may follow strong drink; that continue late into the
> night until wine inflames them! And there shall be
> harp and viol and tabret and pipe (and) wine of their
> feasts; but the deed of the LORD they have not
> regarded, neither have they considered the works of
> His hand. Therefore, My people have gone into
> captivity for lack of knowledge, and the honorable
> men are famished, and their multitude are parched
> with thirst. Therefore, Sheol has enlarged her gullet
> and opened her mouth without measure; and her
> glory and multitude have descended, and her tumult
> and he who exalts in her. (Isaiah 5:11–14)

These are the

Men of Scoffing who are in Jerusalem. (Isaiah 28:14)

Those are they who

have rejected the Law of the LORD, and the Word of the Holy One of Israel they have despised, Therefore is the anger of the LORD kindled against His people, and He has stretched forth His hand against them and has smitten them, and the hills trembled, and their carcasses were as refuse in the midst of the streets. For all this His anger is turned not away, and His hand is stretched out still. (Isaiah 5:24b–25)

That is the congregation of the Men of Scoffing who are in Jerusalem. He has confused the path of … for it is written concerning him in Jeremiah …

Now therefore, behold, the Lord bringeth up upon them the waters of the river, strong and many, even the king of Assyria and all his glory: And he shall come up over all his channels and go over all his banks: And he shall pass through Judah; he shall overflow and go over; he shall reach even to the neck, and the stretching out of his wings shall fill the breadth of your land, O Immanuel.
(Isaiah 8:7–8)

Interpretation: … the law; he is Rezin and the son of Romeliah … as it is written …

As it is written concerning them:

Therefore, the LORD shall set up the adversaries of Rezin against him, and join his enemies together; the

41

Syrians before, and the Philistines behind; and they shall devour Israel with open mouth. For all this His anger is not turned away, but His hand is stretched out still. (Isaiah 9:11–12)

Interpretation: ... and he ...

For the people do not turn to Him that smites them, neither do they seek the Lord of Hosts. Therefore, the LORD will cut off from Israel head and tail, branch and rush, in one day. The ancient and honorable, He is the head; and the prophet who teaches lies [Teacher of Lies], he is the tail. For the leaders of these people cause them to err; and they that follow them are destroyed. Therefore, the Lord shall have no joy in their young men, neither shall have mercy on their fatherless and widows ...
(Isaiah 9:13–17a)

Interpretation: ...

For wickedness burns as the fire: it shall devour the briers and thorns, and shall kindle in the thickets of the forest, and they shall mount up like the lifting up of smoke. Through the wrath of the Lord of Hosts is the land darkened, and the people shall be as the fuel of the fire: no man shall spare his brother. And he shall snatch on the right hand and be hungry; and he shall eat on the left hand, and they shall not be satisfied: they shall eat every man the flesh of his own arm: Manasseh, Ephraim; and Ephraim, Manasseh: and they together shall be against Judah.

For all this His anger is not turned away, but His hand is stretched out still. (Isaiah 9:18–21)

And the rest of the trees of His forest shall be few, that a child may write them. (Isaiah 10:19)

Interpretation: the edict of Babylon … the edict of nations … to betray many …

And it shall come to pass in that day, that the remnant of Israel, and such as are escaped of the house of Jacob, shall no more again stay on him that smote them; but shall stay on the LORD, the Holy One of Israel, in truth. The remnant shall return, even the remnant of Jacob, unto the mighty God. For though Your people Israel be as the sand of the sea, yet a remnant of them shall return. (Isaiah 10:20–22a)

Interpretation: At the End of Days, they will go into captivity. This concerns the reduction of mankind … the "remnant of Israel" is the assembly of His chosen one … the men of His army … the "remnant of Jacob" is … the priests. And since it is written:

the consumption decreed shall overflow with righteousness. For the Lord God of Hosts shall make a consumption, even determined, in the midst of all the land. (Isaiah 10:22b–23)

This is the …

Therefore, thus says the Lord God of Hosts, O My people that dwellest in Zion, be not afraid of the Assyrian: he shall smite you with a rod, and shall lift up his staff against you, after the manner of Egypt. (Isaiah 10:24)

> The great in height will be hewn down, and the lofty will be brought low. The thickets of the forest will be cut down with an axe, and Lebanon by a majestic one will fall. (Isaiah 10:33–34)

Interpretation: The Romans who will beat down the House of Israel and the poor ones … all the Gentiles and warriors will be dismayed, and their hearts will melt … the "great in height will be hewn down" are the Roman warriors. The "thickets of the forest will be cut down with an axe" are … to the Roman war. And "Lebanon by a majestic one will fall" are the Romans who will be given into the hand of this great one … when he flees from before …

> And there shall come forth a Shoot from the stump of Jesse, and a Branch shall grow out of his roots. And the spirit of the LORD shall rest upon Him, the spirit of wisdom and understanding, the spirit of counsel and might, the spirit of knowledge and the fear of the LORD. His delight shall be in the fear of the LORD. He shall not judge by the sight of His eyes nor decide by what His ears hear but He will judge the poor with righteousness and decide with equity for the meek of the earth. He shall smite the earth with the rod of His mouth, and with the breath of His lips He shall slay the wicked. Righteousness shall be the girdle of His waist, and faithfulness the girdle of His loins. (Isaiah 11:1–5)

Interpretation: The Shoot of David who will arise at the End of Days is the Messiah. He will attack His enemies, and God will sustain Him with … a throne of glory, a holy crown, and royal garments. Israel will be protected by Him, and He will rule over all the Gentiles. He shall judge Magog with all those people by the sword. And as it says, "Not judge by the sight of His eyes or decide by what his ears shall hear" means He will judge by the Scriptures, and according to what they teach Him so shall He judge, and according to their command. In agreement with Him, one of the priests with repute shall go out with garments …

Interpretation: This concerns the king of Babylon, since it is written:

Yea, the fir trees rejoice at you, and the cedars of Lebanon, saying, since you are laid down, no feller is come up against us. (Isaiah 14:8)

The fir trees and the cedars represent …

This is the purpose that is purposed upon the whole earth: And this is the hand that is stretched out upon all the nations. For the Lord of Hosts has purposed, and who shall disannul it? His hand is stretched out, and who shall turn it back? (Isaiah 14:26–27)

Woe to the rebellious children, says the LORD, that take counsel, but not Mine; and a covering not of My spirit, that they may add sin to sin: That walk to go down into Egypt, and have not asked at My mouth; to strengthen themselves in the strength of Pharaoh, and to trust in the shadow of Egypt! Therefore, shall the strength of Pharaoh be your shame, and the trust in the shadow of Egypt your confusion. For his princes were at Zoan, and his ambassadors came to Hanes. They were all ashamed of a people that could not profit them, nor be a help nor profit, but a shame, and a reproach. (Isaiah 30:1–5)

Interpretation: Those who sought the sons of Zadok ... which he said to them ...

Therefore, the LORD will wait, that He may be gracious unto you, and therefore will He be exalted, that He may have mercy upon you: for the LORD *is* a God of judgment: blessed *are* all those who wait for Him. For the people shall dwell in Zion at Jerusalem: you shall weep no more: He will be very gracious unto you at the voice of your cry; when He shall hear it, He will answer you. Though the Lord gives you the bread of adversity, and the water of affliction, yet your teachers shall not be removed into a corner anymore, but your eyes shall see your teachers: And your ears shall hear a word behind you, saying, "This is the way, walk in it," when you turn to the right hand, and when you turn to the left. (Isaiah 30:18–21)

Interpretation: At the Last Days, concerning the congregation of the Seekers After Smooth Things who are in Jerusalem ... by the Law and not ... a heart for to seek ...

The chosen ones of Israel ... As it is written:

For the vile person will speak foolishly, and his heart will work iniquity, practice hypocrisy, utter error against the LORD, make empty the soul of the hungry, and he will cause the drink of the thirsty to fail. (Isaiah 32:6)

… the beginning of … who ruled in … the men of the community …

> O you afflicted, tossed with tempest, and not
> comforted, behold, I will lay your stones with fair
> colors, and lay your foundations with sapphires. And
> I will make your windows of agates, and your gates
> of carbuncles, and all your borders of pleasant stones.
> (Isaiah 54:11–12)

Interpretation: All Israel sought You according to Your word. "And I shall lay your foundations in lapis lazuli" means that they have founded the Council of the Community. The "priests and the people" are the Congregation of His Elect, like a stone of lapis lazuli among the stones. "And I will make as agate all your pinnacles" concerns the twelve … giving light in accordance with the Urim and Thummim. Those who "are lacking and not comforted" from them, like the sun in all of its light. The "gates" are the heads of the tribes of Israel at the End of Days …

> They profaned the sanctuary … they arose to battle
> one another against His covenant. God saved and
> delivered … He gave them a single heart to walk in
> the way of His truth … and they abhorred the way of
> wickedness and kept apart from it … the erring spirit
> and with a tongue of truth … their iniquity was
> atoned for through [His] strokes … their iniquity.
> (4Q183)

Ken's Commentary

The term "End of Days" refers to the time right before the end of an Age. Isaiah 5:7 shows oppression came before the Lord sent destruction. It was true for the first century, right before the end of that age, and it will be true before the Second Coming. Notice that, during the End of Days, there will be a reduction of the population of mankind.

Verses 11–15 mention the harp and viol, also called the kinnor and nevel, which are both Hebrew twelve-stringed instruments. These instruments denote the prophecy will be fulfilled in the 12th Onah (AD 1576–2075). If this verse also refers to the time Israel is back in their land, then it is between AD 1948 and 2075. (See Catena A, 3Q177, for a study on stringed instruments.) During the time of the Essenes, the Men of Scoffing were the Sadducees. Today, that term refers to all those who do not acknowledge God in their daily lives.

Verses 19–24 show two captivities, one in Babylon and one in "the nations," due to the expulsion by Rome. The 70-year captivity in Babylon ended in 537 BC. The 1,800-year captivity, decreed by Rome, ended in AD 1948. The End of Days captivity is either the one from Rome or one that will occur shortly, in our time. Tribulation saints need not fear the Antichrist (the Assyrian), because they follow the Lord and are hidden, possibly in Petra.

Verse 30 says woe to those who are covered by a spirit that is not God's Spirit. These are false teachers and false prophets who claim to hear from the Lord and teach in His name but make up foolishness out of their own wicked hearts. The apostle Paul warned about them, saying,

> Having a form of godliness but denying the power thereof: from such turn away. (2 Timothy 3:5 KJV)

Verses 33–34 are talking about either the first-century fall of Israel to Rome or, in this century, Israel's resistance to the revived Roman Empire.

Isaiah 11:1–5 identifies the "Rod of Jesse" as the Messiah.

4Q183 shows the Sadducees and Pharisees left the true faith and even killed each other over false doctrine. Those who love the Lord must step out of the way and let the Lord destroy those who leave the true faith. This is a good lesson for us today to avoid those who want to argue doctrine and call each other heretics. The Essenes' interpretation of Isaiah 53 is that we are spiritually healed by the Messiah's strokes!

Jeremiah (Apocryphon): 4Q384–390

4Q384–385a

... they came to Tahpanhes. Their deeds were just as it was recorded in *The Book of Time Divisions*; with their divisions, families, and tongues, along with the specific sins committed against the Covenant and the guilt of the people ...

Fragment 11

After the seventy years are over, there will be a split between the Way and the people without learning. They will join house to house ...[3]

Fragment 12

Seven hundred [years?][4] ... expel the abomination of the house they did not build ... a period of two years the sons of Israel ...

---

[3] *The New Covenant of Damascus*, pg. 29, predicts that the believing Jews will leave the apostate house of Judah, and the many messianic houses will fellowship together. They believed this is a fulfillment of Micah 7:11.

[4] *The Ancient Book of Enoch* records prophetic history in sets of 700 years. In the sixth set, the "house of dominion" will be burnt with fire. The Jerusalem Temple was burned with fire in AD 70; two or three years later, the Jewish Essene temple in Egypt was shut down. Alternately, the 700 years may refer to the time between Israel's establishment under Moses to the time of the apostasy in Jeremiah's day.

Fragment 15

God will return to His people after the remnant of the flock return when He looses wild beasts [Romans] who conquer the Greeks … They inherit the mountains of Lebanon.

4Q387, 4Q388a, 4Q389
Fragment 1

You said, "our God has left us," but you scorned My statutes, forsook My covenant festivals, and defiled My name and My holy things. You desecrated My temple and sacrificed to the *se'irim*.[5] You violated all these things deliberately and in secret. I looked for faith but could not find any. So, I delivered you into your enemy's hand, and I made the land desolate until it had paid off its sabbaths. You will remain in the lands of your enemies until the year of …

Fragment 2

You will serve Me with all your heart, mind, and soul. They will seek Me in their affliction, but I will not respond to their prayers, because of their past sins. By the completion of ten Jubilees of years, you will again be walking in madness,[6] blind, and bedeviled. After that generation comes to an end, I will rip the kingdom from those who seized it,[7] and I shall raise up over it another people. The

---

[5] The goat-demons (or devils in the KJV) of Leviticus 17:7.

[6] The Pharisee/Sadducee wars of the first century BC and first century AD.

[7] "But from the days of John the Baptist until now, the kingdom of Heaven suffers violence, and the violent seize it." (Matthew 11:12 LITV)

insolent rule over all the land will cause the kingdom of Israel to be lost.

I will hide My face from Israel, and the kingdom will return to many nations. And the children of Israel cry out because of the heavy yoke in the lands of their captivity [Roman besiegement of Jerusalem?] and there will be none to deliver them because they scorned My statutes and abhorred My Torah.

Therefore, I have hidden My face from them until they accomplish their iniquity.[8] And this is the sign to them of the requital of their iniquity, for I shall leave the land because of their haughtiness towards Me, and they will not know that I have spurned them, and they will once again do evil that will be greater than the former evil, and they will violate the covenant which I made with Abraham, Isaac, and Jacob. In those days will arise a Gentile king;[9] who is a blasphemer and commits abominations, and I shall rip his kingdom away, and that king, too, will be a destroyer to other kings. In his days, I shall remove Israel from being a people. In his days, I shall break the kingdom of Egypt, and I shall break Israel and deliver her up to the sword. And I shall lay waste the land, and I shall drive man away, and the priests of Jerusalem will return to idolatry and follow the abominations of the Gentiles ...

---

[8] 537 BC or AD 1948?
[9] Titus?

Fragment 3

<u>Three priests</u> will walk in the ways of the former priests who by the name of the God of Israel were called and, in their days, will be brought down to the pride of those who act wickedly against the covenant and of the slaves of foreign things, and Israel will be rent asunder in that generation, each man fighting against his neighbor over the Torah and over the covenant.

> I will send <u>hunger</u> upon the land, but not for bread or water, but to hear the Word of the Lord.
> (Similar to Amos 8:11)

4Q390

Fragment 1

And before Me and again I shall deliver them into the hand of the sons of Aaron, <u>seventy years</u>. And the sons of Aaron will rule over them, but they will not walk in My ways, which I command you so that you may warn them. And they too will do what is evil in My eyes, like all that which the Israelites had done in the former days of their kingdom, except for those who will come first from the land of their captivity to build the temple. And I shall speak to them, and I shall send them commandments, and they will understand everything which they and their fathers had abandoned. And from the time when that generation comes to an end, in the <u>seventh Jubilee of the deliverance of the land</u>, they will forget statute and festival and Sabbath and covenant. And they will violate everything, and they will do what is evil in My eyes. Therefore, I shall hide My face from them and deliver them into the hands of their enemies; and I shall deliver them up to the sword. But I shall leave among them refugees, so that they should not be annihilated in My wrath and when My face is hidden from them. And the angels of Mastemot [Satan] will rule over them, and I shall spurn them, and they will return to do what is evil in My eyes, and they will walk in the willfulness of their heart.

Fragment 2

And My house and My altar and the Holy of Holies … so it was done … for these things will befall them, and there will be the rule of Belial over them so as to deliver them to the sword for a week of years. And in that Jubilee, they will be violating all My statutes and all My commandments which I shall have commanded them and sent in the hand of My servant the prophets. And they will begin to quarrel among themselves for seventy years, from the day of their violation of the oath and the covenant which they will have violated. So, I shall deliver them into the hand of the angels of Mastemot [Satan], and they will rule over them. And they will not know nor understand that I was angry with them because of their trespass, by which they have forsaken Me and will have done what is evil in My eyes, and what I did not want they will have chosen: To pursue wealth, gain, and violence, each robbing that which belongs to his neighbor and oppressing each other. They will defile My Temple [Mount?], they will profane My Sabbaths, they will forget My festivals, and with foreigners they will profane their offspring. Their priests will commit violence …

4Q389

Fragment 1

Jeremiah son of Hilkiah from the land of Egypt ... The thirty-sixth year of the exile of Israel [571 BC] they read these things before ...

Ken's Commentary

The Jeremiah Apocryphon is a commentary on Jeremiah from the prophecy point of view. Let's look at the different sections.

4Q384–385a mentions *The Book of Time Divisions*. This was a book of prophecy that not only told what was going to happen but listed those events by date in Jubilees (50-year periods) and Shemittahs (seven-year periods). My book, *The New Covenant of Damascus*, explains it this way:

> The explanation of the ending periods, when Israel is blind to all this, is detailed in *The Book of Time Divisions*, in Jubilees, and Weeks.
> (Fragments of Priestly Laws 47)

It also shows that, when the Israelites came back from their 70-year captivity, there was an immediate split between those who served the Lord (followers of the Way) and those who went their own way. The Essene Community left Israel under heavy persecution and dwelt in Egypt until the Romans restored peace by conquering the Greek rulers of Syria and Lebanon to the north. The 700 years might be from 537 BC (when Israel returned from the 70-year captivity) to when the Essenes returned to Israel to prepare the Way for the Messiah.

4Q387, 4Q388a, 4Q389

The priests (Seekers of Smooth Things) apostatized and worshiped demons, specifically the se'irim. Those who returned in 537 BC did seek God, but God left them alone for another 10 Jubilees or one complete Onah (500 years). They returned in the eighth Jubilee of the seventh Onah (575–526 BC). Seven Jubilees later, another apostasy began (225–176 BC). After the 10 Jubilees were finished, in the following Jubilee (25 BC–AD 25), all of Israel was walking in madness. In the next Jubilee, or generation (AD 25–75), God ripped the government from those who seized it (the Pharisees and Sadducees) and gave the kingdom to the Christians. During that same Jubilee, Jesus was crucified, and the Jerusalem Temple was destroyed.

4Q390, Fragment 2

Since we are told that this was read to Israel in the 36th year of their captivity in Babylon, the coming judgment must be future, either toward the first coming or the Second Coming. So, the one week of years (seven years) could be the civil war that occurred between the Pharisees and Sadducees around 90–80 BC. Seventy years prior to that would have been 160 BC, which was right about the time of the Maccabean revolution against Antiochus Epiphanes. If so, it seems to be a type of the Seven-year Tribulation period. Since there is a difference of opinion regarding exactly when the civil war occurred, this might be a direct reference to the Seven-year Tribulation period. I wonder if a quarrel between traditional Jews and Messianic Jews begins exactly 70 years prior to the tribulation period. Or—and this is pure speculation on my part—what if they violated their oath to restore the Temple in AD 1967 by taking control of the Temple Mount and giving control of it back to the Muslims? AD 1967 plus 70 years would be AD 2037. What kind of contention might occur between now and then?

Pseudo-Ezekiel: 4Q385–6, 388, 391

Gentile Destruction - 4Q385

These are the words of Ezekiel. The Word of the Lord came to me and said, "Son of man, prophesy and say, 'The day of destruction for the Gentiles is coming. There shall be anguish in Libya, and the sword shall be in Egypt ... will shake, Ethiopia shall fall, and the mighty of Arabia. Some of the sons of the covenant and Arabia will fall at the gates of Egypt. Lost will be ... by the sword Egypt will be plundered ... where is your portion, O Amon, which dwells by the Nile ... waters surround you, your rampart is the sea, and waters are your wall. Cush, Egypt, is her might, and there is no end to your bars. Libya is your help, yet she shall go into exile, into captivity, and her babies shall be dashed at the head of mountains; and for her princely ones, lots will be cast, and all of her great ones in chains ...'"

4Q385
Valley of Dry Bones - Fragment 2

For I am the Lord who redeems My people, giving unto them the covenant. And I said, "O Lord! I have seen many men from Israel who have loved Your name and have walked in the ways of Your heart. When will these things come to be, and how will they be recompensed for their piety?" and the Lord said to me, "I will manifest to the children of Israel, and they shall know that I am the Lord." And He said, "Son of man, prophesy over the bones and speak, and let them be joined bone to its bone and joint to its joint." And it was so. And He said a second time, "Prophesy and let arteries come upon them and let skin cover them from above." And it was so.

4Q385 – 537 BC

And He said, "Prophesy once again over the four winds of heaven and let them <u>blow breath into the slain</u>." And it was so. And a large crowd of people came to life and blessed the Lord Sabaoth who had given them life. And I said, "O Lord! When shall these things come to be?" And the Lord said unto me: "Until … after days the tree shall bow and shall stand erect …"

4Q386 – AD 1948

And they were covered with skin and arteries came upon them, but <u>there was no breath in them</u>. And He said to me, "Prophesy once again over the four winds of heaven and let them blow into them." And a large crowd of people stood on their feet and blessed the Lord Sabaoth who had given them life.

Then the Lord said to me, "Son of man, tell them … in the place of their burial they will lie until … from your graves … from the land …"

Hastening/Shortening of Days

Make my soul rejoice, and let the days hasten quickly that He said by men, "Indeed, the days are hastening on so that the children of Israel may inherit." And the Lord said to me, "I will not refuse you, O Ezekiel! I will cut the days and the years short, a little as you said ... for the mouth of the Lord has spoken these things."

Son of Belial - 4Q386 Fragment 1.2

"... land and they shall know that I am the Lord." And He said to me, "Look, O son of man, at the land of Israel." And I said, "I have seen, O Lord; and, behold, it lies waste, and when will You gather them together?" And the Lord said, "A son of Belial will scheme to oppress My people, but I will not allow him; and his kin will not survive, nor will there be left from the impure one any seed; and from the grapevine, there shall be no wine, nor will a bee make any honey ... and the wicked one I will slay in Memphis, but My children I will bring forth from Memphis, and their remnant I shall return. As they shall say, 'Peace and tranquility have come,' and they shall say, 'The land shall be as it was in the days of old.' Then I will raise up wrath from the four corners of the heavens ... like burning fire as ..."

Babylon, Fragment 1.3

And on the poor, He will not have mercy, but He wi᾿ ᾿ng them to Babylon. And Babylon will be like a cup hand of the Lord, in her time ... He will cast her ou᾿ Babylon, and it shall be a dwelling place for demon

Filled with the Spirit? Fragment 6

... and My people shall be ... with contented heart and with a willing soul ... and conceal yourself for a little while ... and from divisions ...

Vision of Cherubim

The vision which Ezekiel saw ... a radiance of a chariot, and four living creatures; a living creature ... and while walking they would not turn ... backwards; upon two legs each living creature was walking, and its two legs ... upon ... in one there was spirit, and their faces were one beside the other. And the appearance of the faces, one a lion, one an eagle, one a calf, and one a man, and there was a hand of a man joined from the backs of the living creatures and attached to their wings ... and the wheels ... wheel joined to wheel as they went, and from the two sides of their wheels were streams of fire, and there were in the midst of the coals, living creatures like coals of fire ... and the wheels and the living creatures and the wheels; and there was ... over their heads a firmament like ... the terrible ice. And there was a sound from above the firmament ..."

4Q391, Fragment 25

In your midst will fall all the ... on the earth, and they will elevate Ephraim—will bring up dust ... and over you lame ... and weeping ... to Abaddon ... say to the king ...

... ...

... ace ent 36

and ... of the LORD, and He said ... see and I said to Him ... the bow of the LORD ... the LORD spoke to me, H ... g ... the Israelites ...

Fragment 65

... River Chebar, and I saw ... and I knew that the LORD ... thirteen ... cubits and the height five ... base and the postern is the fifth of ... on the day of one ...

Ken's Commentary

4Q385, Fragment 1, seems to be an End-time scenario. Here, Libya, Egypt, and Ethiopia fall to some power. Daniel says the Antichrist will conquer Egypt, Libya, and Ethiopia. Church father Hippolytus says these three countries are the three of the 10 nations that come against the Antichrist and are destroyed. (See *End Times by the Ancient Church Fathers* pp. 61–62 for more details.)

> He shall stretch out his hand against the countries, and the land of Egypt shall not escape. He shall have power over the treasures of gold and silver, and over all the precious things of Egypt; also the Libyans and Ethiopians shall follow at his heels.
> (Daniel 11:42–43 NKJV)

Since Rome never conquered Arabia, this prophecy has to be about the Antichrist's time. Fragment 1.3 of 4Q386 seems to be referring to Babylon, so we have a comparison of the exile into Babylon and the Antichrist's persecution.

4Q385, Fragment 2, is the Parable of the Valley of Dry Bones we see in Ezekiel 37. What is fascinating is that there are two different versions. I do not think either is a copyist error. The version in 4Q385 states Israel comes back into their land with the Spirit of God. This is exactly what happened in 537 BC under the edict of Cyrus. In the time of Ezra and Nehemiah, they forsook the paganism and went back to serving the LORD with all their heart and with a true understanding of the Messiah. The version in 4Q386 shows they come back into their land and become a nation once again, but without the Spirit. This is the same scenario as the biblical prophecy in Ezekiel 37. This is exactly what happened in AD 1948. Israel is back in the land but under the false assumption that the Messiah did not come in AD 32 as was specifically predicted in Daniel 9. The nation of Israel becomes messianic later, when the "tree" (Israel) "bows down" to serve the Messiah.

This fragment ends with reference to the shortening of days. Compare this to Jesus's words in Matthew:

> For then shall be great tribulation, such as was not since the beginning of the world to this time, no, nor ever shall be. And except those days should be shortened, there should no flesh be saved: but for the elect's sake those days shall be shortened.
> (Matthew 24:21–22 AKJV)

4Q386 refers to a son of Belial (son of Satan) who attacks Israel before God's wrath is poured out. This might be an End-time prediction of the Antichrist, but it could also be speaking of the first coming of the Messiah and the Pharisee/Sadducee movement against the true Essene believers, the sons of Zadok, or both. Notice this happens when they say, "Peace and Tranquility." The apostle Paul said the same thing:

> For when they shall say, Peace and safety; then sudden destruction cometh upon them, as travail upon a woman with child; and they shall not escape. (1 Thessalonians 5:3 KJV)

Fragment 6 may be saying that when Israel accepts the Messiah, the New Covenant of Jeremiah 31 will be placed in their heart. They will no longer have divisions but will be of one mind.

Fragment 6 continues with a description of the Cherubim as seen in Ezekiel 10. Notice that there are references to fire and ice. These are the two judgments of the earth: the flood of water and the destruction by fire. This might help us to understand that the wheel within the wheel may refer to the DSS calendar. If so, this could be giving us a timeframe of the prophecies.

Daniel Commentary: 4Q243–46

4Q242 – Prayer of Nabonidus

The words of this prayer which Nabonidus, king of Babylon, the great king, prayed when he was smitten with a bad disease by the decree of God when he was in Teiman. I, Nabonidus, with a bad disease was smitten for seven years, and since God set His face on me, He healed me; and as for my sin, He forgave it. A Jewish seer, who was from among the exiles, came to me and said, "Proclaim and write to give honor and exaltation to the name of God Most High." And I wrote as follows, "I was smitten by a bad disease when I was in Teiman by the decree of the Most High God. For seven years, I was praying to the gods of silver and gold, bronze, iron, wood, stone, clay, since I thought that they were gods. Apart from them, I was made strong again from what He caused to pass. The peace of my repose returned to me …"

4Q243, Fragments 12, 13, 16 combined with 4Q244

The Israelites chose their ways rather than the presence of God, and they were sacrificing their children to the demons of error/idolatry; and God became angry at them and gave them into the hand of Nebuchadnezzar, king of Babylon, and to make their land desolate of them because … exiles … For seventy years … with His great hand He will save them … powerful … and the kingdoms of the peoples … It is a holy kingdom …

4Q243

Fragment 1
He asked Daniel saying, "On account of …" your God, and a number. He will pray …

Fragment 2
… Daniel before Belshazzar …

Fragment 6
And it was written … Daniel, who …

Fragment 7
The Chaldeans, indeed, the Children of … The way of truth …

Fragment 9
To Enoch …

Fragment 11
Wise men, and he said … Egypt, by the hand of … dominion in the land …

Fragment 24
The sons of evil have led astray … after this, the elect will be assembled … the people, and there will be one from that day … and the kings of the peoples … are doing until this day …

4Q244

Fragment 4
Daniel said …

Fragment 8
After the Flood, Noah from Mount Lubar … a city

Fragment 9
Tower, whose height was …

4Q245, Fragment 1
This book was given … Daniel, Levi, Kohath, Bukki, Uzzi, Zadok, Abiathar, Hilkiah, Onias … Jonathan, Simon … Ahaziah, Joash …

4Q246 – Aramaic Daniel Study
… the spirit of God rested on him [Daniel], he fell down before the throne. … O King, you are angry forever and your years … your vision and all. Forever you … the great ones. An oppression will come to the earth … a great massacre in the provinces … the king of Assyria and Egypt … he will be great on earth … will make and all will serve … he will call himself exulted and designate his name himself. He will be proclaimed the "Son of God" and called the "Son Most High." Their kingdom [the 10 nations] will be like the shooting stars [or sparks] you saw in the vision. They will reign only <u>seven years</u> over the earth. They will crush people as nation tramples nation. Then the people of God will arise, and all will rest from the sword. His kingdom will be an everlasting kingdom [Daniel 7:27], and everyone will walk in truth. They will judge the earth in truth, and all will make peace. The sword will cease from the earth, and all the nations will pay homage to Him. The Great God [Daniel 2:45] will be their help. He will fight for them. He will give the nations into their hands, and all nations will be in their power. His dominion will be an

everlasting dominion [Daniel 7:14] ... and all the boundaries of the earth are His.

Ken's Commentary

4Q242 shows the repentance of Nebuchadnezzar. Some have questioned why the king was called Nabonidus in this text instead of Nebuchadnezzar. I believe that Nebuchadnezzar was the name of the King and that Nabonidus was the title. Notice Daniel was called a seer. This is another name for a prophet.

> Beforetime in Israel, when a man went to enquire of God, thus he spake, Come, and let us go to the seer: for he that is now called a prophet was beforetime called a seer. (1 Samuel 9:9 KJV)

The main parts of 4Q243 and 4Q244 mention the 70-year captivity for Israel in Babylon. One thing it mentions, which our biblical book of Daniel does not, is that they were so incredibly wicked that they sacrificed their children to demons.

There are other very small fragments from 4Q243. One that draws my attention is fragment 9 which mentions Enoch. Since 4Q242 is a commentary on Daniel 4, it looks like 4Q243 contained a commentary on Daniel 2 and 5. If so, the reference to Enoch is most likely connecting the statue of Daniel 2, in which each metal represents an Empire, with Enoch 52 and the *Testament of Noah*, in which the same metals are listed describing those same empires. Daniel 2:31–45 shows gold, silver, copper (bronze), iron, and clay to be Babylon, Persia, Greece, Rome, and a revived Roman Empire. Enoch shows,

> These mountains which your eyes have seen: the mountain of iron, and the mountain of copper, and the mountain of silver, and the mountain of gold, and the mountain of soft metal, and the mountain of lead, all these will melt as wax before fire in the presence of the Elect One.
> (*Ancient Book of Enoch* 52:6)

Revelation described the seven heads of the dragon which represent the seven kings or empires. The *Testament of Noah* has all these together in their proper order. The *Ancient Apocalypse of Ezra* mentions them in this order also.

Scroll 4Q243 mentions these and refers to the Chaldeans (Babylon), Egypt, and others, which were some of the empires.

Scroll 4Q244 mentions Noah's Ark landing and the Tower of Babel. Then 4Q245, fragment 1, mentions "this book." I believe this was the *Book of Enoch*, which was handed down, along with the other books from the pre-flood patriarchs, through the keepers of the ancient scrolls, such as Levi, Kohath, and Zadok, all the way down to Daniel.

Scroll 4Q246 seems to be saying that the Antichrist—who, in Daniel 11, is described as the king of the north (Assyria) who attacks the king of the south (Egypt)—will call himself exalted and arrogantly choose his own title. He will call himself "The Son of God" and "Son of the Most High." His kingdom will only exist for *seven years*. This seven-year period ends with the establishment of the millennial Kingdom of God.

Hosea Commentary: 4Q163, 166–7

> For she did not know that I gave her corn, wine, and oil, and multiplied her silver and gold, which they prepared for Baal. (Hosea 2:8)

Interpretation: They ate and were filled, but they forgot God. They cast His commandments aside which He had sent by the hand of His servants the prophets, and they listened to those who led them astray. They revered them, and in their blindness, they feared them as though they were gods.

> Therefore, will I return and take away My corn in that time, and My wine in its season, and will take back My wool and My flax given to cover her nakedness. And now will I display her lewdness in the sight of her lovers, and no one will deliver her out of My hand. (Hosea 2:9–10)

Interpretation: He smote them with hunger and nakedness that they might be shamed and disgraced in the sight of the nations upon which they relied. They will not deliver them from their miseries.

> I will also cause all her mirth to cease, her feast days, her new months, and her sabbaths, and all her solemn feasts. (Hosea 2:11)

Interpretation: They have rejected the ruling of the Law and have followed the festivals of the nations. But their rejoicing shall come to an end and shall be changed into mourning.

I will destroy her vines and her fig trees, of which she said, "These are my rewards that my lovers have given me." I will make them a forest, and the beasts of the field shall eat them. (Hosea 2:12)

When Ephraim saw his sickness, and Judah saw his wound, then went Ephraim to the Assyrian, and sent to King Jareb: yet could he not heal you, nor cure you of your wound. For I will be like a lion to Ephraim, and as a young lion to the house of Judah: I will tear and go away; I will take away, and none shall rescue him. (Hosea 5:13–14)

Interpretation: Your wound shall not be healed … the furious young lion is the last priest who shall stretch out his hand to strike Ephraim … Ephraim will attack the priest in the "Time of Trial" that is coming. Ephraim, the Jewish renegades of Jerusalem, are led astray but will eventually flee from their false teachers.

I will go and return to My place, till they acknowledge their offence, and seek My face. in their affliction they will seek Me early. (Hosea 5:15)

Interpretation: God has hidden His face from … and they did not listen …

They, like Adam, have broken the Covenant. There they dealt treacherously with Me. (Hosea 6:7)

Interpretation: … they have forsaken God and … according to the decrees of the Gentiles …

Gilead is a city of them that work iniquity and polluted with blood. (Hosea 6:8)

Interpretation: They forsook God and followed the customs of ... them in all ...

And as bands of robbers wait for a man, so the company of priests murder with one consent and commit lewdness. (Hosea 6:9)

Interpretation: At the Last Days, concerning the congregation of the Seekers After Smooth Things who are in Jerusalem ... by the Law and not ... a heart for to seek ...

I have seen a horrible thing in the house of Israel: there is the whoredom of Ephraim, Israel is defiled. (Hosea 6:10)

Interpretation: ... wicked ones of the Gentiles ...

Ken's Commentary

T⁾ʰ⁻ ᵉsene understanding of Hosea is that it is prophetic ₔoₛ ᵃ's time when the Babylonians conquered Israel. ⅃ut it is also a prophecy about their time (the end of the Age ᵣf Torah), when Israel was conquered by the Romans, ᵢon to being about our time (the end of the Age of f. right before the Second Coming. The Sadducees of ₐy (the Seekers of Smooth Things) twisted Torah ᵤmpletely different religion—a cult, basically—and led all who disagreed with them. There will be a ₘ the future when the nation of Israel will Intₒ ledge that they are still following the Sadducee way hₐ ₗl repent. To seek God "early" would be *before* the rejₑ the next millennium (AD 2075). The messianic moᵥ ent in Israel is growing at a fast pace even now.

Micah Commentary: 1Q14, 4Q168

All this is for the transgression of Jacob and for the sins of the House of Israel. What is the transgression of Jacob? Is it not Samaria? And what is the high place of Judah? Is it not Jerusalem? I will make of Samaria a ruin in the fields, and of Jerusalem a plantation of vines. (Micah 1:5–6)

Interpretation: This concerns the Sprouter of Lies who led the simple astray.

And what is the high place of Judah? Is it not Jerusalem? (Micah 1:5b)

Interpretation: This concerns the Teacher of Righteousness who expounded the law to His council and to all who freely pledged themselves to join the elect of God to keep the Law in the Council of the Community, who shall be saved on the Day of Judgment.

Ken's Commentary

I wish we had the rest of this commentary. The Essenes looked at this as the time when the Messiah, the Teacher of Righteousness, would bring salvation, eternal life, to those who freely accept it by confessing (pledging) themselves to join the Community. In other words, they confessed that they were followers of the Messiah and His Way. They confessed they were Christians. The "Sprouter of Lies" are those who teach a different gospel or a different Messiah. We have a lot of that today!

Nahum Commentary: 4Q169

The LORD has His way in the tempest and in the storm, and the clouds are the dust of His feet. (Nahum 1:3b)

Interpretation: The tempest and the storm are from the firmaments of His heaven and of His earth which He has created.

He rebukes the sea and dries it up. (Nahum1:4a)

Interpretation: The sea is all the Romans who ... to execute judgement against them and destroy them from the face of the earth, together with all their rulers whose dominion shall be ended.

Bashan and Carmel wither, and the sprout of Lebanon withers. (Nahum 1:4b)

Interpretation: ... many will perish by it, during the height of wickedness for the ... Carmel and to his rulers. "Lebanon" and the "sprout of Lebanon" are the priests, the sons of Zadok and the men of their council ... they shall perish from before the elect [chosen ones].

The mountains quake before Him, the hills heave, the earth is lifted up before Him, and the world and all that dwell in it. Who can stand before His wrath? And who can arise against His furious anger? (Nahum 1:5–6a)

Interpretation: ... all the inhabitants of the world.

Where is the lions' den and the cave of the young lions? (Nahum 2:11a DSS)

Interpretation: This concerns ... a dwelling place for the ungodly of the nations.

Whither the lion goes, there is the lion's cub, with none to disturb it. (Nahum 2:11b)

Interpretation: This concerns Demetrius, king of Greece [294–288 BC] who wanted to enter Jerusalem on the counsel of the Seekers of Smooth Things. God did not permit Jerusalem to be delivered into the hands of the kings of Greece, from the time of Antiochus until the coming of the Roman rulers. But afterward, Jerusalem shall be trampled under their feet.

The lion tears enough for its cubs, and it chokes prey for its lionesses. (Nahum 2:12a)

Interpretation: This concerns the furious young lion who strikes by means of his great men and by means of the men of his council.

... and fills his cave with prey, and his den with soil. (Nahum 2:12b)

Interpretation: The young Lion of Wrath who fills his cave with prey by executing revenge on the Seekers of Smooth Things and hangs men alive on a tree, which had never been before performed in Israel, for it is a horrible thing to hang one alive on a tree.

Behold, I am against you, says the Lord of Hosts, and I will burn her chariots in the smoke, and the sword shall devour your young lions: and I will cut off your prey from the earth, and the voice of your messengers shall no more be heard. (Nahum 2:13)

Interpretation: "Your chariots" are his bands of soldiers. "Young lions" are his nobles and the members of his council. "His spoils" are the wealth which the priests of Jerusalem accumulated, which they will deliver … Ephraim, Israel, will be given for a … "his messengers" are his envoys whose voice shall no more be heard among the nations.

Woe to the bloody city! It is full of lies and robbery. (Nahum 3:1a)

Interpretation: This city of Ephraim, the Seekers of Smooth Things during the End of Days, walk in lies and falsehood.

The victims never depart, The noise of a whip, and the noise of the rattling of the wheels, and of the prancing horses, and of the jumping chariots. The horseman lifts up both the bright sword and the glittering spear: and many are slain, and a great number of carcasses; and there is no end to their corpses; they stumble upon their corpses. (Nahum 3:1b–3)

Interpretation: This concerns the rule of the Seekers of Smooth Things. The Gentile sword, captivity, looting, burning, exile, and fear of their enemies shall *never* leave their assembly. A multitude of guilty corpses shall fall in their days; there shall be no end to the sum of their slain.

They shall also stumble upon their own "body of flesh [unique sins]" because of their guilty counsel.[10]

> Because of the multitude of the idolatries of the well-favored harlot, the mistress of sorceries, that sells nations through her idolatries, and families through her sorceries. (Nahum 3:4)

Interpretation: This concerns those who lead Ephraim astray, and who will lead many astray by their false teaching, their lying tongue, and deceitful lips—kings, princes, priests, and people, together with the stranger [Gar][11] who joins them. Cities and families shall perish through their counsel; honorable men and rulers shall fall through what they say.

> Behold, I am against you, says the Lord of Hosts; and I will lift up your skirts upon your face, and I will show the nations your nakedness, and the kingdoms your shame. (Nahum 3:5)

Interpretation: … cities of the east. The skirts are… The nations with their uncleanness and their detestable abominations.

> I will cast abominable filth upon you and make you a vile spectacle. And it shall come to pass that all that look upon you shall flee from you. (Nahum 3:6–7a)

Interpretation: This concerns the Seekers of Smooth Things, whose evil deeds shall be uncovered to all Israel at

---

[10] This phrase is quoted in the Damascus Covenant. For a Modern English translation of this scroll see *The New Covenant of Damascus* by this author.

[11] A "Gar" refers to a Gentile believer who never converted to Judaism.

the end of time. Many shall understand their iniquity and treat them with contempt because of their guilty insolence. When the glory of Judah shall arise, the simple of Ephraim shall flee from their assembly; they shall abandon those who lead them astray and shall join Israel.

> They shall say, Nineveh is laid waste; who shall grieve over her? Where shall I seek comforters for you? (Nahum 3:7b)

Interpretation: This concerns the Seekers of Smooth Things, whose council shall perish and whose congregation shall be dispersed. They shall lead the assembly astray no more, and the simple shall support their council no more.

> Are you better than Amon which lay among the rivers? (Nahum 3:8a)

Interpretation: "Amon" is Manasseh, and "the rivers" are the noble men of Manasseh, the honorable of …

> … which was surrounded by waters, whose rampart was the sea and whose walls were waters?
> (Nahum 3:8b)

Interpretation: These are her valiant, mighty warriors.

> Ethiopia and Egypt were her strength, and it was infinite; Put and Libya were your helpers.
> (Nahum 3:9)

Interpretation: These are the wicked of [Judah], the House of Separation [Peleg], who joined Manasseh.

> Yet she was exiled; she went into captivity. Her children were crushed at the top of all the streets.

They cast lots for her honorable men, and all her great men were bound with chains. (Nahum 3:10)

Interpretation: This concerns Manasseh in the <u>final Age</u>, whose hold over Israel will weaken ... his women, children, and little ones shall go into captivity. His mighty men and honorable men [shall perish] by the sword.

You shall be drunk and shall be stupefied. (Nahum 3:11a)

Interpretation: This concerns the wicked of Ephraim ... whose cup shall come after Manasseh ...

You shall also seek refuge in the city because of the enemy. (Nahum 3:11b)

Interpretation: This concerns their enemies in the city ...

All your strongholds are fig trees with young fruit. (Nahum 3:12a)

Interpretation: ...

Behold, the people in your midst are women: the gates of your land shall be set wide open unto your enemies: the fire shall devour your bars. (Nahum 3:13)

Interpretation: The entire region of Israel out to the sea ...

Ken's Commentary

In 4Q169, "Commentary on the Prophet Nahum," the fall of the Roman Empire is predicted. Rome came a long time after the fall of Assyria and Babylon, and they didn't fall in the first century. Instead, Israel fell to Rome, which they acknowledged would happen. So, they are interpreting this to mean the fall of the revived Roman Empire at the end of the Age of Grace just before the establishment of the Kingdom of the Messiah. Revelation has the beast rising out of the sea, which it says is the Gentile nations. If we apply this passage to that, then the beast rises not only from the sea of Gentile nations but *the sea* of a revived Roman Empire.

The commentary of 1:4b gives the outline that the Sadducees started a major persecution of Essenes, which ended in many assassinations.

The commentary of 2:11b says this refers to Demetrius, king of Greece [294–288 BC]. The Sadducees, the Seekers of Smooth Things, pleaded with him to send troops into Jerusalem so that they could maintain complete control over the people. Hmm… a government so corrupt that they fear the people enough to make a pact with an enemy to come and restore their "order." They will remain in power at all costs, even if it means killing their own people. God caused the Grecian Empire to break up into four smaller kingdoms so that they couldn't come as asked. Israel was free after the time of Antiochus Epiphanes and until the coming of the Romans.

I believe that, in the commentary of 2:12, the "lion of wrath" is referring to the rise of the Pharisees who drove back the Sadducees and restored some order but in time became a different kind of governmental perversion. When the Essenes fled to Egypt and left the other two groups to fight among themselves, there was such a vicious war (around 90 BC) that Rome had to step in and restore order. The Essene commentary even predicts the burning of the Temple and Jerusalem, and the expulsion of the Jews, all because of the Sadducees.

The commentary of 3:4 shows that the attitude of "staying in power no matter what and killing off any who oppose them" is one of the main false teachings (called idolatries) of the End-time, well-favored harlot. The proper response is what Gamaliel, Paul's teacher, said,

> Now I say to you, "Withdraw from these men and let them alone. For if this counsel or this work is of men, it will come to nothing. But if it is of God, you cannot overthrow it, lest perhaps you be found even to fight against God." (Acts 5:38–39 MKJV)

The commentary of 3:9–10 reminds us about the tribe of Manasseh separating from Israel by going beyond the Jordan. It resulted in their being the first tribe to be taken by the Assyrians. It compares this to those who leave the true teachings of Scripture and follow a cult like the Sadducees. They will all be the first ones to fall. Anyone who continues to study Scripture and takes it seriously will not become trapped in false doctrine and bloodshed. They created an idiom for this idea, *the House of Separation*. I think it's interesting that the word for separation is "peleg" which means "division" or "an earthquake." Those who cause division will have their lives shaken and destroyed.

The commentary on 3:11, states that those still in the House of Separation (who do not believe that Jesus is the Messiah) that exists in the *last Age* will be stupefied, go into captivity, and perish. Compare this to Zechariah 14:1–4. The Essenes agreed this is a Second Coming prophecy!

Notice that the commentary of 3:12a teaches that fig trees with budding fruit represent perverted strongholds in Israel. Jesus used this idiom to show that the strongholds of the false doctrine of the Sadducees and Pharisees were there in His time, and they would be destroyed. We are to correctly understand Scripture and tear down those strongholds.

For the weapons of our warfare are not carnal, but mighty through God to the pulling down of strong holds: (2 Corinthians 10:4 KJV)

The punishment for walking away from God is destruction. But notice how it comes. The government will, under the guise of compassion, open the border and allow anyone to come in without being vetted, *if* they side with the ruling government. This causes an invasion, and the country is destroyed. This is a typical Sadducee tactic.

Habakkuk Commentary: 1QHab

This concerns the beginning of the *final generation.*

Behold you among the heathen, and regard, and wonder marvelously: for I will work a work in your days which you will not believe, though it be told you. (Habakkuk 1:5)

Interpretation: First, this concerns the unfaithful who followed the Liar and refused to listen to the Teacher of Righteousness, whose words are from the very mouth of God! These are the unfaithful of the New Covenant who have not believed in the Covenant of God, having blasphemed His holy Name.

Second, this also concerns the unfaithful at the End of Days. These men of violence, who are the breakers of the covenant, will not believe when they hear everything that happens in the final generation from the Priest to whom God gave the good news[12] that He might interpret all the words of His servants the prophets, through whom He foretold all that would happen to His people and His land.

For, lo, I raise up the Chaldeans, that bitter and hasty nation, which shall march through the breadth of the land, to possess the dwelling places that are not theirs. They are terrible and dreadful: their judgment

---

[12] The Messiah taught prophecy; see Matthew 24, Luke 21, and Mark 13.

and their dignity shall proceed of themselves.
(Habakkuk 1:6–7)

Interpretation: This concerns the Romans who strike all the nations with fear and dread. They intentionally plot evil and deal with cunning and guile toward all nations.

Are You not from everlasting, O LORD my God, my Holy One? We shall not die. O LORD, You have ordained them for judgment; and, O mighty God, You have established them for correction. (Habakkuk 1:12)

Interpretation: God will destroy His people by means of the Gentiles. But it is by means of His elect that God will execute judgment on all the nations. And it is at the time of their chastisement that all the sinful from amongst His people shall make atonement. Those who will have kept His commandments will be a rock for them ...

Wherefore look upon them that deal treacherously, and hold their tongue when the wicked devours the man who is more righteous than he? (Habakkuk 1:13b)

Interpretation: This refers to the House of Absalom and its supporters, who were silent when the Teacher of Righteousness was punished and did not aid Him against the Liar who had scorned the Law in the midst of all the peoples.

I will stand upon my watch, and set me upon the tower, and will watch to see what he will say unto me, and what I shall answer when I am reproved. (Habakkuk 2:1)

God told Habakkuk to write down what would happen to the final generation, but He did not reveal to him when these events of the final period[13] would be complete. Where he said:

> And The LORD answered me and said, "Write the vision, and make it plain on the tablets, that he who reads it may run." (Habakkuk 2:2)

Interpretation: This concerns the Teacher of Righteousness through whom God made known all the mysteries of the words of His servants the prophets.

> For the vision is still for an appointed time, but it speaks to the end, and it does not lie. (Habakkuk 2:3a)

Interpretation: This means that the final Age shall be prolonged and shall exceed all that the prophets have said, for the mysteries of God are astounding.

> Behold, his soul which is lifted up is not upright in him: but the just shall live by his faith. (Habakkuk 2:4)

Interpretation: This concerns all those who follow the Law of the House of Judah, whom God will deliver from their suffering in the House of Judgment[14] because of their faith in the Teacher of Righteousness.

---

[13] Hebrew word "Dor," meaning a generation, Age, or revolution of time.
[14] Or "House of Damnation."

Also, because he transgresses by wine,[15] he is a proud man, neither keeps at home, who enlarges his desire as hell, and is as death, never satisfied, but gathers unto him all nations, and heaps unto him all people: Shall not all these take up a parable against him, and a taunting proverb against him, and say, "Woe to him that increases what is not his! How long? and to him who lades himself with thick clay!" (Habakkuk 2:5–6)

Interpretation: This concerns the Wicked Priest who was truly called by *HaShem* when he first arose. But when he ruled over Israel, his heart became proud, and he forsook God and betrayed the statutes for the sake of riches.

Will they not rise up suddenly who shall bite you, and awaken to vex you, and you will be for booties unto them? (Habakkuk 2:7)

Interpretation: This concerns the Rebellious Priest who persecuted the Teacher of Righteousness who struck Him during his evil judgment; and stinking profaners committed horrible things to him. This Rebellious Priest violated God's precepts. His wickedness is judged by the infliction of painful diseases that take vengeance upon his fleshly body. And as for that which He said,

Because you have spoiled many nations, all the remnant of the people shall spoil you; (Habakkuk 2:8)

---

[15] Or wealth.

Interpretation: This concerns the last priests of Jerusalem, who shall amass riches by plundering the people. But in their last days, those riches shall be delivered into the hands of the Roman army, for they are "the remnant of the people."

> ... because of men's blood, and for the violence of the land, of the city, and of all that dwell therein. (Habakkuk 2:8c)

Interpretation: This concerns the Wicked Priest who committed crimes against the Teacher of Righteousness and the men of his council. Because of his wickedness against His elect, God delivered him into the hands of his enemies to bitterly humiliate him by means of a *destroying scourge*.

> Woe to him that covets an evil covetousness to his house, that he may set his nest on high, that he may be delivered from the power of evil! You have sent shame to your house by cutting off many people and have sinned against your soul. For the stone shall cry out of the wall, and the beam out of the timber shall answer it. (Habakkuk 2:9–11)

Interpretation: This refers to the Priest who ... so that its stones took part in the oppression and the beam of its timberwork in its theft ... the "many people" is the House of Judgment.[16] For God will give His judgment in the midst of many peoples. In the midst of these, He will condemn it; and by a fire of sulfur, He will destroy it.

---

[16] Or damnation.

Woe to him that builds a town with blood and establishes a city by iniquity! Behold, is it not of the Lord of Hosts that the people shall labor in the very fire, and the people shall weary themselves in vain? (Habakkuk 2:12–13)

Interpretation: This refers to the Lying Prophet who has beguiled many in order to rebuild his town of vanity in bloodshed, and in order that his town should stand to bear witness with deceit by means of its new glory; in order that many might toil in his vain service; in order that they might conceive through deceitful works; in order that their labor might be for nothing; in order that they might come to the judgment of fire for having insulted and outraged the Elect One of God.

For the earth shall be filled with the knowledge of the glory of the LORD, as the waters cover the sea. (Habakkuk 2:14)

Interpretation: … and then knowledge shall be revealed unto them in abundance like the waters of the sea.

Woe unto him who gives his neighbor drink, that puts your bottle to him, and makes him drunken also, that you may look on their nakedness! (Habakkuk 2:15)

Interpretation: This concerns the Wicked Priest who pursued the Teacher of Righteousness to the house of His exile with intense fury to destroy Him by stripping Him of His clothing. At the time appointed for the rest on the Day of Atonement, He appeared before them to condemn them and to rebuke them about the fast day, the Sabbath which was only meant for their rest.

> You are filled with shame instead of glory: drink and
> let your foreskin be uncovered: the cup of the
> LORD's right hand shall be turned against you, and
> a shame will be on your glory. (Habakkuk 2:16)

Interpretation: This concerns the priest whose disgrace
became greater than his glory. For he did not circumcise
the foreskin of his heart but walked in extravagance,
attacking the ones who had nothing. The cup of God's
wrath will destroy him!

> For the violence of Lebanon shall cover you, and the
> spoil of beasts, which made them afraid, because of
> men's blood, and for the violence of the land, of the
> city, and of all that dwell there. (Habakkuk 2:17)

Interpretation: Because of the murder of the Man by the
Wicked Priest, God will smite him; and because of
violence in the land, the city and its inhabitants will be
destroyed. God will pay back the Wicked Priest for what
he did to the poor. For "Lebanon" is the community of the
Yahad.[17] The "beasts" are the simple of heart of Judah who
practice the Law. God will condemn him [the Wicked
Priest] to utter destruction, just as he planned to destroy the
poor. This is the interpretation about where it says,
"Because of murder in the city and violence in the land."
The "city" is Jerusalem, where the Wicked Priest works his
deeds and defiles the Temple of God; and the "violence in

---

[17] A contraction of *Yah* (God) and *Ehad* (one united group), meaning
the true followers of God united by the Holy Spirit. Only found once
in the Bible, in Esther 8:17. Many Gentiles who witnessed Purim
became believers, or *Yahad*. They did not become Pharisees but
Noahides.

the land" is the cities of Judah where he stole the assets of the poor.

> What profits the graven image that the maker thereof has graven it; the molten image, and a teacher of lies, that the maker of his work trusts therein, to make dumb idols? (Habakkuk 2:18)

Interpretation: "What prophet is the idol? An *idol* that someone has made is an image, a source of false teaching, though the maker trusts what he has made."

> Woe to him that said to the wood, Awake; to the dumb stone, Arise, it shall teach! Behold, it is laid over with gold and silver, and there is no breath at all in the middle of it. (Habakkuk 2:19)

Interpretation: Making for himself "gods without a voice." The interpretation of the matter concerns all idols of the peoples that they made to worship and bow to ...

Ken's Commentary

This DSS commentary is unique in that we have almost all the first two chapters of Habakkuk. The Essenes saw it as a prophecy of the final generation, or final Jubilee (50-year period). Again, they believed everything goes in cycles.

Verses 1–5 are about the last generation of their Age of Torah. They predict there would be a false high priest, called the Liar, who rejects the Teacher of Righteousness and rejects His New Covenant. But they also predict events in the last generation of the Age of Grace. There will be those who claim to be followers of the Messiah but are violent. They will twist the New Covenant to make a religion of their own. By the way, the Hebrew word for violence is *hamas*!

Verses 6–7 state this prophecy refers to the Roman Empire. Verse 6 is the only place in Habakkuk that uses the Hebrew word Cashdim (כשדים). We translate it "Chaldeans." I think they are saying that, if we remove the middle letter shin, which causes the "d" to become a "t" it becomes the word Kittim (כתים), which means Romans. They are saying that just as it referred to the Babylonian Empire in Habakkuk's time, it also refers to both the Roman Empire of their time and to the revived Roman Empire in the last generation.

Verse 13 is sobering. Those who knew better but did not side with the Messiah when He was put to death will be judged for their silence! We can never turn a blind eye to what is going on. They created an idiom for this kind of person, the *House of Absalom*.

The commentary on 2:3a seems to indicate that the prophecy happens at an appointed time, a festival such as Passover, but during the last generation. One might think that the "prolonging of the final generation" means that the Second Coming is not at the end of the Age of Grace but sometime afterwards, but this cannot be the proper interpretation, because the commentary on Ezekiel clearly says those days will be shortened. So, this probably means that the prophecies from both the Bible and from the

School of the Prophets will be *completely* finished by the end of the Age of Grace.

The commentary on 2:4 clearly says we are justified by what the Messiah would do when he comes. This agrees with Paul's understanding in Galatians 3. Those who follow the House of the Law of Judah hold to the original teaching about the Messiah (see the chapter on 11Q13 for all that entails). Those who are of the House of Bondage were the Sadducee and Pharisee camps back then. Now, they are the denominations who do not take Scripture and its prophecy literally and seriously.

The commentary on 2:5–6 teaches that either Annas or Caiaphas was serious about serving the Lord but got prideful and caught up in politics and corrupted himself. This is a good lesson for all of us. Also, this is probably the earliest use of the term *HaShem*, meaning "the name," to refer to God.

The commentary on 2:7 says that because the wicked Priest attacks the Messiah, he is smitten with a horrible disease. We remember Herod died with a painful disease in his body.

In 2:8c the wicked persecute not only the Messiah but all Christians as well. It mentions the Roman destruction as the *destroying scourge*. Many think this same reference in Isaiah 28:15,18 refers to Jesus's time and our own time (both the "covenant with death, and with hell" and the "overflowing scourge").

Verses 9–11 remind me of what Jesus said in Luke19:

> And He answered and said to them, I tell you that if these should be silent, the stones would cry out. (Luke 19:40 MKJV)

Verses 12–13 show we need to be careful not to fall for the very persuasive and descriptive stories cult leaders tell us today.

The commentary for verse 15 records a time when the wicked priest pursued the Messiah to Qumran. The "House of His Exile" refers to the term "House of the Blood Heir," *Dam Meseq* (דמ משק) in Hebrew. It was their name for Qumran. In English, it would be New Damascus or the House of Damascus (בית דמשק). To strip one "of clothing" is an idiom for stripping "of his rank or authority." They were going to arrest Jesus. It was not His time, so He "showed Himself," and that ended it. This Hebrew word "*Yapha*" is used in the Old Testament for God revealing Himself, like in a theophany or Christophany. Here are a few occurrences: Ps. 94:1, God "shows Himself;" Ps 50:2, "God shined;" Ps 80:1, God "shined" from between the Cherubim over the Mercy Seat. This shows that the Teacher of Righteousness revealed His glory as God incarnate at Qumran. This was probably something like what happened on the Mount of Transfiguration.

The commentary on 2:18 is very important. Even though Sadducees and Pharisees would have nothing to do with an idol statue, they were considered idolators in the eyes of the Essenes because they departed from the ways of God and created a religion in their own image. Today, if we call ourselves Christians but teach false doctrines, we are idolaters. We are held accountable if we attend a cult instead of a real church.

Zephaniah Commentary: 1Q15, 4Q170

And it shall come to pass at that time, that I will search Jerusalem with candles and punish the men that are complacent, who say in their heart, The LORD will not do good, neither will He do evil. Therefore, their goods shall become a booty and their houses a desolation: they shall also build houses, but not inhabit them; and they shall plant vineyards, but not drink the wine. (Zephaniah 1:12–13)

Interpretation: They shall not eat … "their wealth shall be plundered" means … in the fire of His jealous wrath, all the earth will be consumed.

For He shall make a complete, yea, a speedy end of all those living in the land. (Zephaniah 1:18b)

Come together and hold an assembly, O shameless nation, before you are driven away like chaff, a day has passed away, before the fierce anger of the Lord comes upon you. (Zephaniah 2:1–2)

Interpretation: This concerns all those who dwell in the land of Judah …

Ken's Commentary

I believe this would again be understood as the time when God's visitation occurred and Israel was found evil and totally corrupt. It was then destroyed. It will be corrupt again when they accept the Antichrist.

Zechariah Commentary: 4Q163

And it was broken in that day: and so the poor of the flock that waited upon Me knew that it was the Word of the LORD. Then I said to them, "If it is agreeable to you, give Me My wages; and if not, refrain." So they weighed out for My wages thirty pieces of silver. (Zechariah 11:11–12)

Interpretation: Those who sought the sons of Zadok …

Ken's Commentary

Zechariah 11 is speaking of the time when the covenant between God and Israel is broken. It was when the Messiah was betrayed for 30 pieces of silver. I believe it was saying that the sons of Zadok, the Essenes, had separated themselves from the ruling Jews and were the only ones still in covenant with Messiah.

Malachi Commentary: 4Q253a

Then those fearing the Lord spoke with one another, and He heeded and heard them, and a *Book of Memorial* was written before Him of those who feared the Lord and meditated on His name. They shall be Mine, says the Lord of Hosts, My jewels <u>on the day when I act</u>, and I will spare them as a man spares his son who serves him. Then once more you shall distinguish between the righteous and the wicked, between one who serves God and one who does not serve Him. (Malachi 3:16–18)

Interpretation: … the righteousness and upon … and he who is a man from Israel who …

Ken's Commentary

There is not much commentary here. The text adds the phrase "on the day when I act" which is not in the Hebrew version of Malachi 3. This predicts a remnant of believing Jews who follow Messiah but are confused. At the proper time, recorded in the Book of Memorial, God will choose them, and they will follow Him as true sons.

Chapter 2 of the *Damascus Document* tells of the Essenes reassembling after major assassination attempts. They prayed for guidance, and there was a Christophany. The Messiah told them of His plans and ordered them to go to Egypt until it was safe. This was three years before Antiochus Epiphanes rose to power. This seems to keep happening. The Lord warns believers, they obey, and the ones who ignore the warning get slaughtered. This is what happened with the Maccabees; and in AD 68, it was what happened to the Christians that left for Pella. In the days to come, believers must focus on prophecy or they may perish.

Prophecy Studies

11QMelchizedek: 11Q13

Column 2

Moses said, "In the year of the Jubilee, each of you will be freed to return home [Lev. 25:13]," and he described how, saying, "Now this is the manner of the release: Let every creditor [Baal] remit what he has lent his neighbor. He shall not press his neighbor or his brother for repayment, for the LORD's release has been proclaimed [Deut. 15:2]." Its interpretation pertains to the End of Days. The captives Moses speaks of are those of whom Isaiah says, "To proclaim freedom to the captives [Isa. 61:1]." Its interpretation is that the LORD will assign those freed to the sons of heaven and the lot of Melchizedek, even those whose teachers had deliberately hidden and kept secret from them the truth about their inheritance through Melchizedek. The LORD will cast their lot amid the portions of Melchizedek, who will make them return [or repent] and will proclaim freedom to them, to free them from the debt of all their iniquities. This event will take place in the first week of the Jubilee that occurs after the ninth Jubilee [AD 32].

Now the Day of Atonement is the end of the tenth Jubilee [AD 75], when atonement (is made) for all the sons of heaven, for the men of the lot of Melchizedek … It is the time of Melchizedek's "Day of Grace." He will, by His strength, raise up the holy ones of God to execute judgment as it has been written concerning Him in the songs of David, as it says, "Elohim stands in the divine assembly; in

101

the midst of Elohim, He judges [Psalm 82:1]." He said, "Above it, to the heights, return. God will judge the nations [Psalm 7:8–9]." When He said, "How long will you judge unjustly and show impartiality to the wicked? Selah [Psalm 82:2]." Its interpretation concerns Belial and the spirits of his lot who turn away from the commandments of God in wickedness. Melchizedek will exact the vengeances of the judgments of God ...

This is the "Day of Peace" about which God spoke through Isaiah the prophet [52:7] who said, "How beautiful on the mountains are the feet of the Messenger who proclaims peace, the Messenger of good who proclaims salvation, saying to Zion, 'Your God reigns!'" Its interpretation is that the mountains are prophets' predictions about the Messenger, and the Messenger is the One anointed of the Spirit about whom Daniel said, "Until Messiah, the Prince, there will be seven weeks ... [Dan. 9:25]." He is the Messenger of good who proclaims salvation. He is the One about whom it is written, when it says, "to comfort those who mourn ... [Isa 61:2–3]" to "instruct them in all the periods of the Ages in truth."

Zion is those who uphold the covenant, those who turn aside from walking in the ways of the people. But "your God" is Melchizedek, who will save them from the hand of Belial. As for that which He has said, "You will blow the signal-horn in the seventh month [Lev. 23:24 or 25:9]." ... the divisions of the times ...

Column 3, Fragments 3, 7, 8

... two hundred ... the week ... the division of times ... At its appointed time ... the end of the Jubilee ... he will carry it ... Melchizedek ... the hands of ...

Ken's Commentary

This is a compilation of prophecies from Isaiah 52 and 61, Psalms 7 and 82, and Daniel 9. It consists of three columns. Only a few words and letters are visible in the first column, and the third is badly fragmented and cut off. But the second column is nearly perfect. It teaches us about the Messiah and His two comings. Here are the prophetic passages it quotes:

> How beautiful on the mountains are the feet of Him proclaiming good news, making peace heard, bearing tidings of good, making heard salvation, saying to Zion, "Your God reigns."
> (Isaiah 52:7 LITV)

> The Spirit of the Lord GOD is upon Me, Because the LORD has anointed Me To preach good tidings [Gospel] to the poor; He has sent Me to heal the brokenhearted, To proclaim liberty to the captives, And the opening of the prison to those who are bound; To proclaim the acceptable year of the LORD... (Isaiah 61:1–2 NKJV)

> A Psalm of Asaph. God stands in the congregation of the mighty; He judges among the gods. How long will you judge unjustly, And show partiality to the wicked? Selah. (Psalms 82:1–2 NKJV)

> Know therefore and understand, that from the going
> forth of the command to restore and build Jerusalem
> until Messiah the Prince, There shall be seven weeks
> and sixty-two weeks; The street shall be built again,
> and the wall, even in troublesome times.
> (Daniel 9:25 NKJV)

This is about *the* Melchizedekian priest who, in paragraph
3, is the Messiah of Daniel 9:25. Paragraph 4 makes it very
clear that the Messiah is also God incarnate. With the
understanding that the Messiah is the Melchizedekian
priest who is God incarnate, let's go through this
compilation from the beginning.

Paragraph 1 says that the Mosaic Law of forgiving debt on
every Jubilee year (once every 50 years) is a prophetic
symbol that the Messiah would forgive our debts in the last
Jubilee (of the Age of Torah, which was AD 25–75). It goes
on to say that our "debts" are not monetary but are our sins.
It refers to the forgiveness of our sins! His salvation is the
"freeing of the captives" of Isaiah 61. There will be those
Pharisees who deliberately hide the truth about the Messiah
from their people. Even though that happens, His salvation
is still available to everyone, including them. The
paragraph ends by telling us when the Messiah will pay for
our sins (by His death on the Cross). It will be one
Shemittah (seven years) after the end of the ninth Jubilee
(50-year period) of their Onah (500-year period). When we

convert their calendar to ours, it comes out to AD 32.[18] The Messiah dies for our sins in AD 32!

Paragraph 2 teaches that when the Messiah brings salvation, it will also start the "Day of Grace," which is also called the "Day of Peace." By the end of that Jubilee (AD 75), vengeance will be complete, and the unbelieving government of the nation of Israel will be no more.

Paragraph 3 says that the "Day of Peace" is a name for what Isaiah 61 describes. The prophets' predictions (mountains of prophecy) predict that the Messiah (the Messenger) will bring salvation because He is God incarnate. Notice also that He will teach the truth about the lost calendar and its prophecies (all the periods of the Ages).

After telling us that the Messiah is God incarnate, paragraph 4 begins to teach on the completion of the Age of Grace. It reveals that the Mosaic Law of the trumpet blast in the seventh month is also a symbolic prophecy. This is the Festival of the Awakening Blast on what is called Rosh Hashanah.

Many of us believe the rituals of the fall festivals teach about the Rapture, tribulation period, and Second Coming, just as the Passover Seder teaches about the death, burial, and resurrection of Jesus Christ during the first coming.

---

[18] See dsscalendar.org and the book, *Ancient Dead Sea Scroll Calendar*, for details about how the original God-given calendar works.

This brings us to column 3, which is highly fragmented, but we can gain some understanding about this ritual. The time of the awakening blast (Rapture/Resurrection) has something to do with a week (seven-year period). It is carried out by the hands of the Messiah Himself. It looks like it is toward the end of the Jubilee period, and it seems to be at an appointed time or a messianic festival, such as Rosh Hashanah.

Don't you wish we had the rest of column 3?

Blessed is the man who does not walk in the counsel of the ungodly, nor stand in the way of sinners, nor sit in the seat of the scornful. (Psalm 1:1)

Interpretation: This concerns those who depart from The Way ... which is written in the Book of Isaiah the prophet about the Last Days,

For the LORD spoke thus to me with a strong hand, and instructed me that I should not walk in the way of this people, saying ... (Isaiah 8:11)

And they are those about whom it is written in the Book of Ezekiel the prophet,

Neither shall they defile themselves any more with their idols, nor with their detestable things, nor with any of their transgressions: but I will save them out of all their dwelling places, wherein they have sinned, and will cleanse them: so shall they be My people, and I will be their God. (Ezekiel 37:23)

These are the sons of Zadok and the men of their counsel, who seriously seek justice and have come into the council of the community.

Why do the nations rage and the people imagine a vain thing? Kings of the earth rise up and princes conspire together against the LORD and against His Messiah. (Psalm 2:1–2)

Interpretation: The nations and rulers will come against the Elect of Israel in the Last Days.

This is the "time of the trial" that is coming on Judah to complete ... Belial, and a remnant will remain ... for the lot, and they put the whole Law into practice ... Moses. As it is written in the book of Daniel the prophet,

> The wicked act wickedly and the righteous shall be made white and be purified.
> (Daniel 12:10 and 11:35)

> And a people who know God will remain strong.
> (Daniel 11:32)

After the trial which is for them ... when He descends ... wickedness when ... Israel and Aaron ... know that He ... among the seers ...

Fragment 4

> ... those who devour the offspring of ... furious against them in their zeal. (similar to Isaiah 26:11)

Interpretation: This refers to the time when Belial will open great difficulties upon the house of Judah to create enmity between them. ... he will seek to scatter them with all his might ... who will bring them to ... Judah and to Israel ...

Ken's Commentary

This first section is about those in Israel who follow the true Messiah. It uses several Hebrew words usually just translated "foreigner." There are *Nochri*, who are unbelievers who live a very sinful lifestyle. The *Zurim* are Gentile nations or empires who want to invade and conquer. The *Gar* are Gentiles who know about the Lord but may not be serious about their relationship with Him.

These types of people will never again be a problem to Israel. He will do this through one of King David's descendants. Satan's (Belial's) plan was to cause division by twisting doctrine and creating denominations who would kill people who do not submit to them.

David's descendant, the Messiah, would come though his seed and inherit his House, or throne, and be established as the eternal ruler. God the Father will call the Messiah "His Son," and the Messiah would call God the Father "My Father." The Messiah is the one who is called the Branch of David by Isaiah 11:1; Jeremiah 23:5, 33:15; and Zechariah 3:8. The Messiah will restore the true Law of God which was replaced by the Pharisees' and Sadducees' perverted law. This was prophesied in Amos 9:11, and the apostles stated it was fulfilled in Acts 15:16.

Psalm 1:1 refers to those who call themselves followers of Messiah (the Way) but hold to false doctrine, such as the Pharisees and Sadducees. All this perverted doctrine will be gone in the Millennial reign.

Psalm 2 is about the nations attacking the Messiah at the end of the "Time of Trial," which we call the seven-year tribulation. During this time, Israel will repent and accept the true Messiah which fulfills the prophecies in Daniel 11:32–35 and 12:10.

Notice it says the Second Coming (the descent) will occur at the end of the seven-year tribulation (the Time of Trial).

It ends by reminding us that the main tactic of Satan is to create division among believers and, if possible, cause them to hate each other and kill those who are not part of their denomination or cult.

Messianic Apocalypse: 4Q521

Fragment 2, Column 2

The Heavens and the earth will listen to His Messiah, and none of them will turn away from the commandments of His holy ones [apostles, Essenes]. Seekers of the Lord,[19] strengthen yourselves for His service! Preserve hope in your heart and you will see the Lord! Because the Lord will search for the humble[20] and call the righteous by name. His Spirit will hover upon the humble, and His power will renew the faithful. And He will glorify the humble on the throne of the eternal Kingdom. He will liberate the captives, restore sight to the blind, straighten the bent-down [twisted]. Forever I will remain with those who hope in Him and await His mercy. His Messiah will not be slow in coming. For the Lord will do wonderous things which have never been done before when He comes. He will heal the wounded, revive the dead, and bring good news [Gospel] to the poor [humble]. He will lead the uprooted ones [called out ones] and feed the hungry.

Fragment 2 Column 3

The law of Your grace will free them from [their errors when the] hearts of the fathers return to the sons. ... with the blessing of the Lord in His grace ... may the earth rejoice in every place ... for all Israel in the rejoicing ...

---

[19] "Seekers of the Lord" as opposed to the "Seekers of Smooth Things."
[20] "pious" means devoted (heart holiness), humble, poor in spirit.

113

Fragment 7

... see everything that the Lord has made, the earth and all that is in it, the seas and all that are in them, and all the lakes and rivers ... those who do the good before the Lord ...[21] Those who curse [Him] are destined for death when the Life-Giver will raise the dead of His people. We will give thanks and proclaim to you the righteousness of the Lord, who ... and opens ... He reveals them ... and the path to the abyss ... the accursed have hardened ... and all the angels of the heavens have ...

Ken's Commentary

In contrast to the last chapter, the Synagogue of Satan hates and kills while the Messiah looks for those who are humble. Jesus called this being "poor in spirit." They will obtain eternal life.

Then it gives signs of what the Messiah will do when He comes:

1. He will liberate the captives,
2. restore sight to the blind,
3. straighten the bent-down (twisted),
4. heal the wounded,
5. revive the dead,
6. bring good news (Gospel) to the poor (humble),
7. and fill His seekers with His Spirit.

Compare this to the passage where Jesus was asked by the disciples of John if there was another Messiah.

---

[21] Compare Enoch 1–6; Both Enoch and the Ezra apocalypse use the example of rivers and streams to teach God's timing.

114

Jesus answered and said unto them, Go and shew John again those things which ye do hear and see: The blind receive their sight, and the lame walk, the lepers are cleansed, and the deaf hear, the dead are raised up, and the poor have the gospel preached to them. (Matthew 11:4–5 KJV)

Many have said Jesus is referring to several Old Testament passages like Psalm 146 and Isaiah 61:

... who brings justice for the oppressed, and who gives food to the hungry. The LORD frees the prisoners; the LORD gives sight to the blind. The LORD lifts up those who are weighed down. The LORD loves the righteous. (Psalm 146:7–8 ISV)

The Spirit of the Lord GOD is upon Me, Because the LORD has anointed Me To preach good tidings to the poor; He has sent Me to heal the brokenhearted, to proclaim liberty to the captives, And the opening of the prison to those who are bound. (Isaiah 61:1 NKJV)

While it is true several of these points are in those passages, nowhere in the Old Testament does it predict the Messiah would raise the dead—resurrect them on Judgment Day, yes; but nothing about raising the dead like Elijah did.

In the book, *Ancient Order of Melchizedek*, we show that John the Baptist was an Essene and ran his own school. Since that is the case, we know John would have been very familiar with the Essene commentaries. I believe Jesus is quoting 4Q521 in Matthew 11. John would have instantly known Jesus was telling him Essene theology was correct,

115

which means there would only be one Messiah and He, Jesus, was fulfilling all the predictions listed in this scroll!

It goes on to tell us Jesus will create and lead the "uprooted ones."

In Greek, this became the "called-out ones," *ecclesia*, or the Church. There is little difference between "called-out ones" or "uprooted ones." They both come out of the world, and both are raptured or resurrected.

Fragment 2 column 3 shows that the grace of Jesus saves us when we repent and return to proper doctrine about the Messiah. It also links this to what Elijah does when he returns for the first half of the tribulation period.

> Behold, I will send you Elijah the prophet before the coming of the great and dreadful day of the LORD: And he shall turn the heart of the fathers to the children, and the heart of the children to their fathers, lest I come and smite the earth with a curse. (Malachi 4:5–6 KJV)

Fragment 7 revealed that the Messiah will raise His own to eternal life but throw those who curse Him into the Abyss.

Testimonia (Messianic Anthology): 4Q175

The Lord spoke to Moses saying,

> ... I have heard the voice of the words of this people, which they have spoken to you: they have well said all that they have spoken. O that there were such a heart in them, that they would fear Me and keep all My commandments always, that it might be well with them, and with their children forever! (Deuteronomy 5:28–29)

> I will raise them up a Prophet from among their brothers, like to you, and will put My words in His mouth; and He shall speak to them all that I shall command Him. And it shall come to pass, that whoever will not listen to My words which He shall speak in My name, I will require it of him. (Deuteronomy 18:18–19)

Of Balaam's Oracle,

> And he took up his parable, and said, Balaam the son of Beor has said, and the man whose eyes are open has said, "He has said, which heard the words of God, and knew the knowledge of the Most High, which saw the vision of the Almighty, falling into a trance, but having his eyes open, 'I shall see Him, but not now: I shall behold Him, but not near: there shall come a Star out of Jacob, and a Scepter shall rise out

117

> of Israel, and shall smite the temples of Moab, and
> destroy all the children of Sheth.'"
> (Numbers 24:15–17)

Of Levi,

> And of Levi he said, "Give Your Thummim to Levi
> and Your Urim to Your holy one, whom You tested
> at Massah, and with whom You quarreled at the
> waters of Meribah; Who said to his father and to his
> mother, 'I do not know you'; neither did he
> acknowledge his brothers, nor knew his own
> children: for they have observed Your Word, and
> kept Your covenant. They shall teach Jacob Your
> precepts and Israel Your Law: they shall put incense
> before You, and whole burnt sacrifice on Your altar.
> Bless, LORD, his power, and delight the work of his
> hands; smite the loins of them that rise against him,
> and of them that hate him, that they rise not again."
> (Deuteronomy 33:8–11)

When Joshua finished offering praise and thanksgiving, he
said,

> … Cursed be the man who rebuilds this city, Jericho!
> May he lay its foundation on his first-born and set its
> gate upon his youngest son. (Joshua 6:26)

Behold, an accursed man, one of Belial, arises to become a
fowler's trap to his people, and a destruction to all his
neighbors. And his brother arises, ruling with lies, both
being instruments of violence. They rebuild this city and
erect a wall and towers to make it a stronghold of
ungodliness and wickedness in Israel, and a horror in

Ephraim and in Judah. They commit an abomination in the land, and great blasphemy among the sons of Jacob. They shed blood like water upon the ramparts of the daughter of Zion and within the precincts of Jerusalem.

Ken's Commentary
This scroll quotes Deuteronomy, Numbers, the *Testament of Levi*, and Joshua to show several points of Essene theology.

The Prophet whom God will raise up, whom we must obey, is the Messiah. He is the Star out of Jacob and the Scepter that rises out of Israel. This scroll has "temples of Moab," whereas the KJV has "corners of Moab." I believe we are to take from this that the Messiah will destroy all the corrupt doctrine and false religions when He sets up His kingdom.

Those who reject the Messiah are like those who rebuilt Jericho, even when told not to. They are rebellious even to the point of murdering those who disagree with them.

Catena A: 4Q177

Section 1

As it is written concerning them in the book of Psalms,

> To the chief Musician upon Sheminith [eighth], A Psalm of David. Help, LORD; for the godly man ceases; for the faithful fail from among the children of men. (Psalm 12:1)

For instruction to a people without knowledge. They are the <u>eighth Onah</u> ... compassion ...

> The words of the LORD are pure words: as silver tried in a furnace of earth, purified seven times. (Psalm 12:6)

As is written in the book of the prophet Zechariah,

> For behold the stone that I have laid before Joshua; on one stone shall be seven eyes: behold, I will engrave the engraving thereof, said the Lord of Hosts, and I will remove the iniquity of that land in one day. (Zechariah 3:9)

Section 2

... as is written about them,

> Thus said the Lord GOD, Because Moab and Seir say, Behold, the house of Judah is like to all the heathen. (Ezekiel 25:8)

The interpretation of the word concerns the Last Days when "Judah" comes against a just people, with all zeal and hostility. These wicked and demented simpletons are the congregation of the Seekers After Smooth Things. God will declare them, and all that belongs to them, unclean. The "purified ones" are the men who serve God, who have circumcised the foreskin of their heart in the Last Generation.

Section 3

The Lot of Light mourn during the reign of Belial, the one who rules over the Lot of Darkness ... Those who rebel against the spirits of Belial will be forgiven forever, and He will bless them forever and will record their names by the _Onahs_ of their fathers, according to the number of their names, according to the precise list of their names, of each man individually, their years and the period of their service and their tongues ... the descendants of Judah. And now, see, everything has been written on the tablets which ... and taught him the number of all the _Onahs_ and gave him an inheritance ...

Section 4

The Messenger of His Truth will rescue all the Sons of Light from the power of Belial ... to scatter them in a dry and desolate land. This is the Time of Trouble that ... Continually, the just man will flee, and God's great hand will be with them to deliver them from all the spirits of Belial ... those who reverence and sanctify God's name will enter Zion with joy, and Jerusalem ... Belial and all the men of his lot will be destroyed forever, and all the Sons of Light will be regathered together ...

Ken's Commentary

Section 1 of 4Q177 is very important for students of prophecy. In our calendar chapter, we discussed that they believe all of human history fits into fourteen *Onahs*, or fourteen 500-year periods of time. Their time, when Jesus was here on earth, was the eighth *Onah*.

They are saying that when David wrote Psalm 12, he was prophetically speaking about the first-century Sadducee rulers who were doing all the hate and bloodshed. You can know this for sure because, in the title of the Psalm, it mentions it was to be played on a *Sheminith*, which is an eight-stringed musical instrument. The idea is if a Psalm is prophetic and there is a stringed musical instrument mentioned in the title, then the number of strings of that musical instrument points to the Onah when the prophecy will occur.

The Bible mentions a book of prophecy written by Nathan the prophet in 2 Chronicles 9:29. Only fragments of it are available today; but if we compare this with one of these fragments, we find a teaching that says the titles of the Psalms contain prophecy. Nathan says,

> And when I realized that they had debated for too long, I told them, "This is unsatisfactory, so we will go together to the Tabernacle of God, and we will assemble the degrees of the altar, and upon whom the Spirit of God descends will tell us the order of the book Psalms." Everyone accepted this condition, and we went to the Tabernacle of the Lord. The son of

Korah climbed the first degrees of the altar and spoke, but he did not receive a [prophetic] word, and so he stepped down. Asaph went in turn, and the Spirit of God descended on him, convicting him that neither he nor the son of Korah should complete this task. I went then, and the Spirit of God descended upon me and never left me until the point I had the titles and the recitation formulas for each of the fifteen degrees. The crowd cried with one voice, "This prophecy [the Ascent Psalms] must be attributed to David. It is for him to write it." I said, "No, but each should write each of his psalms in his own name." He [the son of Korah?] fled because of what I said. Then I got up and went to the mountain. I fasted, and I spoke to God with humble prayers until He came to me and gave me all the prophecies which reveal the coming of the Messiah. I wrote them in this volume, and I placed it in my library which is in my capital [Gibeon] ...

(Fragment of *The Book of Nathan the Prophet*)

Notice that the prophet Nathan understood not only that it was very important that each psalm had the correct title in it but that it was connected to the prophecies about the Messiah. The "recitation formulas" are most likely the number of the *Onahs* in the titles. Nathan also wrote several other prophecies about the Messiah (including one about His virgin birth). I hope one day someone finds and excavates ancient Gibeon and finds the complete copy of Nathan's Testament.

This idea that the *Onahs* show when a prophecy will be fulfilled is mentioned several times in the *Ancient Covenant of Damascus*. But let me give you one small example of it from Amos about our time. We are living in the 12th *Onah*, which should end with the Second Coming. A 12-stringed instrument is called a *neval*.

> ... go down to <u>Gath of the Philistines</u>: be they better than these kingdoms? Or their border greater than your border? Ye that put far away the evil day, and cause the <u>seat of violence</u> to come near; That lie upon beds of ivory, and stretch themselves upon their couches, and eat the lambs out of the flock, and the calves out of the midst of the stall; That chant to the sound of <u>the viol</u> ... (Amos 6:2–5 KJV)

In Amos 6, we see that there is an enemy of Israel that is the "seat" or power, meaning the government, of a country called Gath of the Philistines. This is the present-day Gaza Strip. This government calls itself "violence." The Hebrew word for violence is "hamas." They chant to music played on the viol. The Hebrew word translated "viol" in the KJV is a *neval*, which is a 12-stringed musical instrument. If this government is able to cause problems for Israel, then Israel must be a nation. Israel became a nation again in AD 1948, during *Onah* 12. There are other prophecies about the Hamas war and how it ends, but this is just one example of understanding the seasons of time for prophecies by understanding the *Onahs*.

Section 2 tells us that there will be types of Sadducees with hatred and bloodshed toward the followers of the Messiah just because they have a different idea on a particular point of doctrine. Those types of people are still here in the Last Days. This hatred will be at its worst during the last generation of the Last Days. The last generation or Jubilee of *Onah* 8 was when Jesus came (AD 25–75), the Jerusalem Temple was destroyed, and thousands of people were slaughtered. The last Jubilee of our Onah will be AD 2025–2075. You must get ready by accepting Jesus Christ as your Savior!

Section 3 tell us that those evil ones are the sons of Satan (Belial). They are also called the "Sons of Darkness" or the "Lot of Darkness." Believers with a pure heart are the "Sons of Light" or the "Lot of Light." If a Son of Darkness repents, he is forgiven and welcomed into the Lot of Light.

Section 4 tell us about the time when the Sons of Light will finally be permanently rescued from Satan. This occurs during the Tribulation, called here the "Time of Trouble."

Smaller Fragments

The Word: 4Q422

He made the heavens and the earth, with all their host, by His Word.

Ken's Commentary

All creation was made by the Word of God. The "Word of God" is a phrase used throughout Scripture to point to the Messiah.

> In the beginning was the Word, and the Word was with God, and the Word was God. The same was in the beginning with God. All things were made by Him; and without Him was not any thing made that was made. (John 1:1–3 KJV)

Elect One: 4Q534 (4QMess)

He is the Elect One of God. His birth and the expiration of His breath [His death] are ordained by God … His plans will last forever.

Ken's Commentary

They correctly understood that both the birth and death of the Messiah was part of God's plan.

Coming of Elijah: 4Q558

The eighth as an elected one ...

> I will send to you Elijah, before the coming of the great and dreadful day of the LORD with power, lightning, and fire from heaven. (Malachi 4:5)

Ken's Commentary
Since the prophet Elijah lived during the seventh Onah, this might be predicting that he would return during the eighth Onah to usher in the Messiah (the Elect One). This would have been John the Baptist. We are currently in the Onah of the Second Coming, which is the 12th Onah. Notice they add that the Day of the Lord comes with "power, lightning, and fire."

Enoch's 10 Weeks Commentary: 4Q247

Then the fifth week will come ... four-hundred and eighty years [after the Exodus] Solomon built the temple ... It was destroyed during the reign of Zedekiah, king of Judah, and it was restored by the Levites and the people of the Land. It will be destroyed by the king of the Romans ...

Ken's Commentary

This is thought to be a commentary on Enoch's "10 Weeks" Prophecy from Enoch 93. The fifth week was 1125–425 BC. The Essenes understood that the Romans (Kittim) would destroy the Jerusalem Temple. We see also in Daniel 11:33 that the Romans would burn down the Jerusalem Temple.

Seven-Fold Light: Hymn 15

You have made me a father to the Sons of Grace, and a stepfather to the Men of Wonder … I shall shine in a seven-fold light in the council …

Ken's Commentary

The "10 Weeks" Prophecy in Enoch 93 has some sort of seven-fold wisdom/light that is rediscovered around AD 900. Maybe this pertains to some scrolls discovered at that time that are now in the hands of private collectors. If so, I hope we will gain access to them soon.

No Need for Priests: Hymn 14

Because You will bring Your glorious salvation [Yeshua] to all the men of the council, to those who share a common lot with the Angels of the Presence, they will have no need of priests to pray for them, nor prophets to give God's reply. When the scourging flood advances, it shall not invade the stronghold.[22]

Ken's Commentary

Believers in the Messiah do not need priests to pray for them, nor prophets so that they can hear from God. This is definitely a change in dispensations. Again, we have a mention of the "scourging flood" that is coming, but it does not touch believers—maybe because, this time, we are at the Marriage Supper of the Lamb.

Study the Ages: 4Q298

You who are wise and have knowledge, listen! Add to your knowledge, self-control, modesty, and proper judgment. Men who know the Way love patience, truth, righteousness, brotherly kindness, and humility,[23] study the appointed times by which you will understand the end of the Ages, and study the Ancient Words to know ...[24]

Ken's Commentary

We are to study the festivals because they teach prophecy: Passover, Unleavened Bread, First Fruits, Pentecost, New Wine, New Oil, Trumpets, the Day of Atonement, and

---

[22] I would guess that the stronghold is Qumran, but it appears to have been invaded or at least abandoned. Maybe they mean that the scrolls will not be destroyed by the scourge.

[23] Compare to 2 Peter 1:5–7.

[24] Compare to 2 Peter 1:16–21.

Tabernacles. If we study them, we will come to understand ancient prophecies and the times of the Ages. We are also to study the "Ancient Words," which might be a reference to the Testaments, like the "Words of Gad the Seer." This scroll also reminds me of the fruit of the Spirit mentioned by Paul,

But the fruit of the Spirit is love, joy, peace, longsuffering, gentleness, goodness, faith, meekness, temperance: against such there is no law.
(Galatians 5:22–23 KJV)

and the virtues mentioned by Peter,

And beside this, giving all diligence, add to your faith virtue; and to virtue knowledge; And to knowledge temperance; and to temperance patience; and to patience godliness; And to godliness brotherly kindness; and to brotherly kindness charity. For if these things be in you, and abound, they make you that ye shall neither be barren nor unfruitful in the knowledge of our Lord Jesus Christ.
(2 Peter 1:5–8 KJV)

Gaza Plague: 4Q468g

A great plague will infect their bodies. Edom, Gaza, Ashkelon, the sons of Keturah, the remnant of … He will wage war against the cities of Israel and …

Ken's Commentary

The "he" might be the Antichrist. Edom is southern Jordan. Ashkelon is Israeli territory north of Gaza, and Gaza is currently Hamas territory. It is thought that the sons of Keturah intermingled with the Ishmaelites. If so, they are some of the Arab peoples.

Book of War: 4Q285

Fragment 7

As it is written in the book of Isaiah the prophet,

> The thickets of the forest shall be cut down with an axe, and Lebanon shall fall by a majestic one. (Isaiah 10:34)

And

> There shall come forth a shoot from the stump of Jesse, and out of his roots a sapling will grow. (Isaiah 11:1)

This is the "Branch of David," that they will enter into judgment with. The prince of the congregation shall put the Branch of David to death by piercing and wounds. And the high priest will command … the slain of the Kittim …

Ken's Commentary

This fragment of the *Book of War* records that the Messiah is the Branch of David prophesied in Isaiah 11 and that He will be tried and convicted by the "prince of the congregation," which is the High Priest. The Messiah will be pierced and wounded (for our transgressions) and handed over to the Romans for execution.

The Messiah, Branch of David: 11Q14

Fragment 1.1

The Bud of David ... the prophet Isaiah:

> the thickets of the wood will be cut with iron, and Lebanon in its magnificence will fall. (Isaiah 10:34)

> And a shoot will emerge from the stump of Jesse, and a Branch will spring up from its root ... (Isaiah 11:1)

This is the Bud of David. And they shall judge ... and the prince of the congregation shall kill the Bud of David ... [with piercings] and with wounds. And the high priest shall command ... the dead of ...

Ken's Commentary

This is the same text and interpretation as 4Q285. Multiple copies in different caves must mean this passage was a very important prophecy to them.

The Messiah is the "Bud of David" and the "Branch of David" who will be turned over to the Romans by the "Wicked Priest" to be pierced and wounded, fulfilling Isaiah 53, Psalm 22, and Zechariah 12.

> But He was <u>wounded</u> for our transgressions, He was <u>bruised</u> for our iniquities: the chastisement of our peace was upon Him; and with His <u>stripes</u> we are healed. (Isaiah 53:5 KJV)

For dogs have compassed Me: the assembly of the wicked have enclosed Me: they pierced My hands and My feet. (Psalms 22:16 KJV)

Jesus said this was about Him,

And again, another scripture saith, They shall look on Him whom they pierced. (John 19:37 KJV)

End-Time Nephilim: 4Q530

… after two of them had the same dream; and they awoke and came and told their dreams in the assembly of their brothers. The *Elioud*[25] … In the dream, I was watching this very night, and there was a garden. And gardeners were watering two hundred trees, and large shoots came up out of the roots and drained off all the water. And a fire burned up the whole garden.

Ken's Commentary
The "Book of Giants" is a collection of scrolls that give more history about the preflood world and the Nephilim wars, which are briefly mentioned in Genesis 6.

This fragment of the "Book of Giants," 4Q530, records a prophetic dream about the corruption of the 200 angels— the very corruption which led to the Flood. In the dream, the 200 angels are seen as trees in a garden. Many shoots are coming up out of their roots, which signifies many genetic variants of Nephilim. As in the other dreams, the Flood comes and wipes away all the corruption, leaving only Noah and his descendants, as they were of pure blood.

What is particularly interesting about this one fragment is that "gardeners" make sure some of the shoots "drain off" the overflow of water. These shoots survive the destruction

---

[25] A preflood clan of Nephilim. See our book, *Ancient Book of Enoch* for details.

of the waters and are destroyed much later in a coming fire. This seems to indicate that some Nephilim seed, or at least their technology, made it through the Flood and will be destroyed at the Second Coming. Jesus said,

> But as the days of Noah were, so also will the coming of the Son of Man be. (Matthew 24:37 NKJV)

If this is the correct interpretation of the dream, it would explain the giants in Canaan during the time of Moses and Joshua. Several scrolls give us the warning that, in the End Times, we need to trust in the Essene herbal medicine because modern medicine becomes corrupted. This corruption seems to be the same type of genetic tampering of the old days. To heed this warning, we need to be very careful with any modern medicine that alters our genes.

The Teacher of Righteousness

This chapter taken from *The New Covenant of Damascus*.

It is consistent throughout the Old Testament and the New Testament that the Messiah is referred to as the Teacher of Righteousness and the Sun of Righteousness, and that He comes in two separate comings. His first coming is referred to as the former rain, and His Second Coming is referred to as the latter rain. Using different calendars, they both occur in the first month. One occurs in the spring and one in the fall. When referring to the two comings of the Teacher of Righteousness, James says,

> Be patient therefore, brethren, unto the coming of the Lord. Behold, the husbandman waiteth for the precious fruit of the earth, and hath long patience for it, until he receive the early and latter rain.
> (James 5:7 KJV)

James is quoting the prophecy of the comings of the Messiah from Joel:

> Be glad then, children of Zion, and rejoice in the LORD your God: for He has given you the Teacher of Righteousness [*Morah Zedek*], and He will descend for you as the rain, as the former rain, and the latter rain in the first month. (Joel 2:23*)*

We see the same description of the Messiah as the Teacher of Righteousness by the prophet Hosea:

> Sow yourselves in righteousness, reap in mercy; break up your fallow ground: for it is time to seek the

LORD, until the Teacher of Righteousness [*Yorah Zedek*] comes to you. (Hosea 10:12)

A few chapters back, Hosea mentioned the Messiah would come as the "former and latter rains" using the same phrase as the prophet Joel did:

Then shall we know, if we follow on to know the LORD: His going forth is prepared as the morning; and He shall come unto us as the rain, as the latter and former rain unto the earth. (Hosea 6:3 KJV)

The prophet Malachi used the same type of phrase but described the Messiah as the "Sun of Righteousness":

But unto you that fear My name shall the Sun of Righteousness arise with healing in His wings; and ye shall go forth and grow up as calves of the stall. (Malachi 4:2 KJV)

The Dead Sea Scrolls have numerous references to the Messiah as the "Teacher of Righteousness" and as the "Sun of Righteousness." Many "scholars" today keep repeating the idea that the title refers to the person who started the Essene movement about 197 BC. But the scrolls consistently use the title to refer to the coming Messiah. Here are just a few quotes.

Gad the Seer 1

The Messiah is pictured as a lamb in the Sun, while Israel, as a misled nation, is pictured in the moon. The Messiah who comes to grant us salvation and change us into the "Redeemed" is the Sun of Righteousness.

The Habakkuk Commentary – 1QpHab

The Habakkuk Commentary records that, during the time of the Roman occupation of Israel (64 BC to AD 135), the Teacher of Righteousness was persecuted by the Liar. The people of this apostate priest "followed the Liar and refused to listen to the Teacher of Righteousness." They were the "unfaithful of the New Covenant who have not believed in the Covenant of God." These people would be destroyed by the Roman army toward the end of the Age. This wicked priest, the Liar, "committed crimes against the Teacher of Righteousness and the men of His Council." So, they persecuted the Essenes/Christians. How could the same man have started the Essene movement in 197 BC and still have been alive in AD 32?

The very first sentence in the Habakkuk Commentary tells us it is referring to the last generation of their Age. The word for generation relates to the 50-year period known as a Jubilee. So, the Teacher of Righteousness should have started His ministry, died, and begun the new congregation between AD 25 and AD 75. The commentary on Psalm 37 says,

> ... the Wicked Priest who watched the Teacher of Righteousness to kill Him because of the ordinance and the law which He sent to him.

Later it says,

> At the end of the forty years, they shall be blotted out, and the wicked shall no longer be found in the land of Israel. (Commentary on Psalm 37 – 4Q171)

Another Dead Sea Scroll Psalm commentary says,

supplications from the Teacher of Righteousness, the true priest at the end of the Age.
(Commentary on Psalms 127, 129, 118 – 4Q173)

The Dead Sea Scroll commentary on Micah says,

> This concerns the Teacher of Righteousness who expounded the Law to His council and to all who freely pledged themselves to join the elect of God to keep the Law in the Council of the Community, who shall be saved on the Day of Judgment.
> (Commentary on Micah – 1Q14, 4Q168)

The *Damascus Document* says the following about the Unique (or only begotten) Teacher of Righteousness,

> From the day when the Unique Teacher dies, to the destruction of all the warriors who followed the Liar will be about forty years. (*Damascus Document* 14)

> They adhere to the laws of the ancients by which children of men were governed and listen to the voice of the Unique Teacher of Righteousness, never rejecting any of the statutes of the Teacher of Righteousness when they hear them.
> (*Damascus Document* 15)

The Testament of Simeon says the Messiah is both God and man:

> My children, obey Levi, and in Judah will you be redeemed. Do not rebel against these two tribes, for from them will arise the salvation of God. For the Lord will raise up from Levi as it were a Priest, and from Judah as it were a King, who is both God and

man. So, He will save all the Gentiles and Israel. (*Testament of Simeon* 7)

The Testament of Levi says the Messiah is the sun:

His star will arise in heaven, as a king shedding forth the light of knowledge in the sunshine of day, and He will be magnified in the world until His ascension. He will shine forth as the sun in the earth and will drive away all darkness from the world under heaven, and there will be peace in all the earth. The heavens will rejoice in His days, the earth will be glad, and the clouds will be joyful.
(*Testament of Levi* 18)

The Testament of Judah says the Messiah is the God of Righteousness and the Sun of Righteousness:

He is the "Salvation [Yeshua] of Israel" that will come at the "appearing of the God of Righteousness." (*Testament of Judah* 22)

After these things will a star arise to you from Jacob in peace, and a Man will rise from my seed, like the Sun of Righteousness, walking with the sons of men in meekness and righteousness, and no sin will be found in Him. The heavens will be opened above Him to shed forth the blessing of the Spirit from the Holy Father. He will shed forth a spirit of grace on you. You will be to Him sons in truth, and you will walk in His commandments, the first and the last. This is the Branch of God Most High, and this is the well-spring unto life for all flesh. Then the scepter of my kingdom will shine forth, and from your root a stem will arise. In it will arise a Rod of

Righteousness to the Gentiles to judge and to save all that call upon the Lord. (*Testament of Judah* 24)

The Testament of Asher says the Messiah is God incarnate.

You will be disregarded in the Dispersion as useless water until the Most High will visit the earth. He will come as man, eating and drinking with men, and in peace He will break the head of the dragon through water. He will save Israel and all nations, God speaking in the person of man. Therefore, teach these things to your children, so they will not disobey Him. (*Testament of Asher*)

The Testament of Benjamin says the Messiah is the Unique, or "only begotten," One:

The Most High will send forth His salvation in the visitation of His Only-Begotten One.
(*Testament of Benjamin* 9)

The Testament of Aaron says the Messiah is the "Eternal Sun":

His Word will be as the Word of heaven, and His teaching will be in accordance with the will of God. His eternal sun will burn bright. The fire will be kindled in all the corners of the earth. It will shine into the darkness. (*Testament of Aaron* column 4)

The apostle Peter says the Messiah is the "Day Star":

We have also a more sure word of prophecy; whereunto ye do well that ye take heed, as unto a light that shineth in a dark place, until the day dawn, and the Day Star arise in your hearts:
(2 Peter 1:19 KJV)

11QMelchizedek – 11Q13

This scroll refers to the Messiah as the final Melchizedekian priest to come in the Last Days. It says, "Melchizedek is God!" and that when He comes, He will pay the penalty for "our sin nature, reconciling us to God." And this event occurs exactly one *Shemittah* (7-year period) after the end of the ninth Jubilee (50-year period) of their Age. They were at the end of the eighth *Onah* (500-year period) from Creation. On our calendar, that comes out to be AD 32!

Conclusion

The Melchizedekian Priest, Sun of Righteousness, Teacher of Righteousness, Rod of Jesse, is none other than the Messiah, God incarnate, who died for our sins in AD 32. His death was about 40 years before the temple was destroyed.

Summary of Prophecies

Here is a summary of the prophecies about the Dead Sea Scrolls themselves.

1. They are a fulfillment of Isaiah 29 and Daniel 12.
2. The prophecies are based on the Dead Sea Scroll calendar.
3. We are to study the Ages (calendar) to learn prophecy.
4. Most prophecies will occur in the final Jubilee, or generation, of an Age.
5. There is a long list of prophets that wrote prophecy books.
6. They date-predicted events by years, *Shemittahs* (seven-year periods), and Jubilees (50-year periods).
7. The Psalms teach prophecy about the Messiah.
8. We should study Enoch's writings.
9. Preflood books were handed down to Levi.

Here is a summary of the first-coming prophecies from these Dead Sea Scrolls.

1. Messiah comes after Rome removes the sovereignty of Israel.
2. Messiah is called the "Branch of David."
3. Messiah is called the "Shoot of David."
4. Messiah is called the "Rod of Jesse."
5. Messiah is called the "Son of God."
6. Messiah is called the "Elect One."
7. Messiah is called the "Word of God."

Ancient Prophecies from the Dead Sea Scrolls

8. Nathan predicted the virgin birth of Messiah.
9. A Wicked High Priest is the Liar who puts Messiah to death.
10. Messiah dies about 40 years before the Temple is destroyed.
11. Messiah is the Teacher of Righteousness.
12. The just live by faith by believing in the Messiah.
13. Messiah is God incarnate.
14. Messiah dies, then resurrects.
15. Messiah dies to pay for our iniquities.
16. Messiah pays for our sins by His stripes, wounds, and being pierced.
17. Messiah dies for us in AD 32.
18. Messiah ends the Age of Torah and begins the Age of Grace.
19. Messiah is the Prince mentioned in Daniel 9:25.
20. Messiah fulfills Isaiah 11, 52, 53, and 61.
21. Messiah will restore the true Law of God.
22. Messiah teaches prophecy (Matthew 24, Luke 21, Mark 13, etc.).
23. Messiah will liberate the captives, heal the blind, heal the twisted and wounded, raise the dead, and bring the Gospel to the humble.

Here is a summary of the Second Coming prophecies from these Dead Sea Scrolls.

1. Israel would come back in 1948, not understanding the two comings of the Messiah.
2. There will be false Christs and false religions in the Last Days.

3. There will be a messianic movement in Israel.
4. Messiah destroys the armies of Magog.
5. Days will be shortened in the End Times.
6. Israel will have the Urim and Thummim in the End of Days.
7. During the End of Days, there will be a population decrease.
8. Two "Sons of New Oil" will oppose the Antichrist.
9. Antichrist will be connected with the Tribe of Dan.
10. The Antichrist will call himself the "Son of God."
11. The Antichrist will call himself the "Son of the Most High."
12. The Antichrist will rule for seven years.
13. Messiah descends after the Time of Trial.
14. The seven-year rule of the Antichrist will end at the start of the Millennium.
15. When Israel accepts the Messiah, the New Covenant [Jeremiah 31] will be placed in their heart.
16. Nephilim medicine will return.

Definitions

Age of Creation: The first 2,000 years of human history (from Creation to the call of Abraham, when he was 52).

Age of Torah: The second 2,000 years of human history (from the call of Abraham to the destruction of the Temple and the Council of Yavneh, AD 75).

Age of Grace: The third 2,000 years of human history (AD 75–2075).

Age of the Kingdom: This is predicted to be only 1,000 years long. It starts after the Age of Grace and is when Messiah rules on earth (AD 2075–3075).

Beasts/Sheep: The simple that are easily led astray.

Branch of David: The Messiah.

Congregation of the Humble: Those who follow Messiah and refuse violence.

Destroying Scourge: The Romans destroying Jerusalem at the end of the Age of Torah; and the troops of the Antichrist flooding Jerusalem at the end of the Age of Grace.

Elect One: The Messiah.

Ephraim and Manasseh: Other terms for the House of Separation.

Final Generation: The last Jubilee (50-year period) of an Age.

House of Absalom: Those who claim to be believers but refuse to stand with the Messiah.

House of Judah: Also called the *House of the Law of Judah*. This refers to those who hold to the original Mosaic Law and follow the Messiah.

House of Judgment: Those whom God condemns and will judge.

House of Separation: Those who claim to be believers but separate themselves from the assembly.

House of Stumbling: Those who separate from the true faith, like the House of Separation, but they create cultic doctrines that cause the simple to fall.

Interpreter of Knowledge: Same as the Interpreter of the Law.

Interpreter of the Law: The Essene leader who correctly understood the prophecies about the Messiah, John the Baptist.

Just Live by Faith: Salvation comes only though trusting the Messiah.

Liar: The Wicked Priest.

Rebellious Priest: The Wicked Priest.

Life-Giver: The Messiah who resurrects the dead.

Lying Prophet: The Wicked Priest.

Idol: An image or statue that is worshiped or a set of false teachings that lead you away from the Messiah.

Men of Scoffing: Sadducees and others like them who try to deny true doctrine and true prophecy.

Season of Repentance: The 40-year period to engender repentance, which also causes severe persecution of believers.

Seekers of the Lord: Those who follow the Messiah with a circumcised heart. They are the opposite of the Seekers of Smooth Things.

Seekers of Smooth Things: Sadducees, those who believe in nothing but power at all costs.

Sons of Darkness: Pharisees, those who say they believe in a Messiah but knowingly change doctrine to suit themselves.

Sons of Light: Essenes, followers of the Messiah.

Sprouter of Lies: The Wicked Priest, and those like him, who try to discredit the Messiah and his council/church.

Tabernacle of David That Has Fallen: The true teachings about the Messiah that were confused by ancient cults, as predicted by Amos 9:11 and restored in Acts 15:16.

Teacher of Righteousness: The Messiah.

Time of Trial: A seven-year period of tribulation that ends at the establishment of the Messianic Kingdom.

Time of Trouble: Another title for the Time of Trial, the seven-year tribulation period.

Two Sons of Oil: The two witnesses. This is somehow connected to the Festival of New Oil and prophecy.

Violent of the Covenant: Those who claim to be followers of Messiah but fight for their own way, to the point of killing others who disagree with them.

Wicked Priest: The one who had the Messiah put to death.

Word of God: The Messiah.

Yahad: The Yahad are those who are one in the Spirit who serve Messiah with a humble heart.

Index of Scrolls

Other Books by Ken Johnson

- **Ancient Post-Flood History**
  Historical documents that point to a biblical Creation.

- **Ancient Seder Olam**
  A Christian translation of the 2,000-year-old scroll.

- **Ancient Prophecies Revealed**
  500 prophecies listed in order of when they were fulfilled.

- **Ancient Book of Jasher**
  Referenced in Joshua 10:13; 2 Samuel 1:18; 2 Timothy 3:8.

- **Third Corinthians**
  Ancient Gnostics and the end of the world.

- **Ancient Paganism**
  The sorcery of the fallen angels.

- **The Rapture**
  The pretribulational Rapture of the Church viewed from the Bible and the ancient church.

- **Ancient Epistle of Barnabas**
  His life and teaching.

- **The Ancient Church Fathers**
  What the disciples of the apostles taught.

- **Ancient Book of Daniel**

- **Ancient Epistles of John and Jude**

Ancient Prophecies from the Dead Sea Scrolls

- **Ancient Messianic Festivals**
  And the prophecies they reveal.

- **Ancient Word of God**

- **Cults and the Trinity**

- **Ancient Book of Enoch**

- **Ancient Epistles of Timothy and Titus**

- **Fallen Angels**

- **Ancient Book of Jubilees**

- **The Gnostic Origins of Calvinism**

- **The Gnostic Origins of Roman Catholicism**

- **Demonic Gospels**

- **The Pre-Flood Origins of Astrology**

- **The End-Times by the Church Fathers**

- **Ancient Book of Gad the Seer**

- **Ancient Apocalypse of Ezra**
  Called 2 Esdras in the KJV.

- **Ancient Testaments of the Patriarchs**
  Autobiographies from the Dead Sea Scrolls.

- **Ancient Law of Kings**
  Noahide law.

- **Ancient Origins of the Hebrew Roots Movement**
  The Noahide and Mosaic Laws as seen in the Dead Sea Scrolls.

- **Ancient Origins of Modern Holidays**

154

- Ancient Dead Sea Scroll Calendar
- Ancient Order of Melchizedek
- New Covenant of Damascus

Please visit BibleFacts.org for additional details.

Bibliography

Eerdmans Publishing, *Ante-Nicene Fathers*, Eerdmans Publishing, 1886

Whiston, William, *The Works of Flavius Josephus*, London, Miller & Sowerby, 1987. Includes Antiquities of the Jews.

Ken Johnson, *Ancient Messianic Festivals*, Independent publisher, 2012

Ken Johnson, *Ancient Book of Jubilees*, CreateSpace, 2013

Ken Johnson, *End Times by the Ancient Church Fathers*, Independent publisher, 2016

Ken Johnson, *The New Covenant of Damascus*, Independent publisher, 2022

Ken Johnson, *Ancient Book of Enoch*, CreateSpace, 2012

Ken Johnson, *Ancient Order of Melchizedek*, Independent publisher, 2020

Ken Johnson, *Ancient Testaments of the Patriarchs*, Independent publisher, 2017

Ken Johnson, *Ancient Book of Jasher*, CreateSpace, 2008

Ken Johnson, *Ancient Dead Sea Scroll Calendar*, Independent publisher, 2019

Made in the USA
Las Vegas, NV
04 July 2024

91867409R10089